)any

)logues

by Clay Franklin

Foreward by Greer Garson

SAMUEL
FRENCH
FOUNDED 1830
New York Hollywood London Toronto
SAMUELFRENCH.COM

MIXED COMPANY

FOREWORD

The art of the monologist surely must be as old as time, and we can imagine the Life of the Party entertaining his friends and family in firelit caves or sunlit groves with Imitations and Impressions.

Clay Franklin now presents another of his collection of character sketches which should be a delight to reader and performer alike. A kindly sense of humor and acute observation illumine his gallery of recognizable contemporary portraits. Professional performers and drama students will pounce on this lively material and non-pros should try reading them aloud to the home audience. Have fun.

GREER GARSON

INTRODUCTION

Doing a monologue is like playing a game of Let's Pretend—for the solo actor and the audience. Although the setting is announced, it must be imagined —whether it be a fashionable veranda or a crude cabin. The only furniture required for some of these sketches are a chair and small table. It isn't necessary for the actor to wear a costume appropriate to the character. If the characterization is convincing, your audience can readily believe you are dressed in tatters or the latest out of *Vogue*. Simple props such as a telephone, book, newspaper, and cigarette should be used to add to the reality. At the same time the handling of such props gives the actor more ease. To complete the stage picture, the characters to whom the actor speaks and reacts must be imagined before your eyes as actor so that they can be projected to the imagination of your audience.

No specific directions are given when the character should move, sit, rise, etc. Such action is left to the discretion of the actor or teacher. After reading the sketch several times, he should sense when movement is necessary and what vocal interpretation is required.

These sketches should prove of special value to the student actor. There is a responsibility in taking the stage alone—to realize that he must be immersed in a role from start to finish—and that no other fellow actors are there to help him put over a scene. There is no quicker method of gaining versatility—to be able to portray a variety of roles, with various dialects perhaps—than to perform a monologue.

May you enjoy getting acquainted with the following characters, whether they are used for armchair reading, auditions, class-room presentations, or performances on a stage before an audience.

CONTENTS

MIXED COMPANY

THE TELEPHONE AND SALLY

It is shortly after a school session as Sally scampers into her living room, tosses aside a text book and purse, crosses to the telephone and dials a number. During her chat she sprawls in the various contortions on chair and floor that only agile teenagers can accomplish.

Kay? . . . Hi. Sally. Give a listen to this. Guess who asked me for a movie date tonight? . . . Phil Sands? I couldn't care less. Try again. . . . Funny girl. Tom Winters is a stuffed piece of conceit—with pimples. . . . Natch, it's someone dreamy. . . . All right, I'll give. Ken Walker. There. Did you flip? I think he's absolutely the most!

It happened right after biology class. I looked up and there was Ken walking beside me. He started to talk about the poison glands in a lizard. And before we got to history—a date. Whee, was I on a pink cloud!

Kay, you don't mind if I borrow your beige skirt, do you? It'll look peachy with that yellow cashmere sweater and the lemon yellow blouse. . . . Don't be ridic. I don't have them. But Elsa Harding has the sweater. She has my saddle shoes since last month. Sue Little has the blouse. She didn't borrow a thing. I'll gush about the speech she made today—and that should do it. So if I may pick up your skirt— . . . What? . . . Kay, you didn't! All over it? . . . I'm sure it looks lovely with ketchup polka dots.

Now what'll I do? I wanted to wear something different tonight. After the movie we'll probably hop over to the Down Beat for a dance or two. . . . And how do you know he's an awful dancer? You never— . . . Oh, that one. Betsy Willard brags about more dates than are in the history book. So all right. If Ken doesn't care to dance we can drop by for a snack somewhere.

Look, Kay, I better breeze off and call Elsa about her sweater. Oh weepers. Her yellow and my navy skirt will look gruesome. I'll be doubled in two. Now who has a beige skirt? . . . Phyllis Jordan. Oh, I'd never ask her for a pin. She's prima donna herself ever since she's been in that class play. I'll ring Liz Ward. She has clothes for every minute of the day. 'Bye now.

Hi, Mother. When did you come home? Oh. I'll do that errand in a minute, Mother. I'm putting through a call to Liz. It's urgent—practically an emergency.

Hello. Is that you, Liz? . . . Oh. Hi, Don. Is your sister around? . . . Thank you . . .

Hi, Liz. I hope your brother's voice will change soon. He sounds just like you. Liz, may I ask a stupendous favor? Have you something to go with a yellow blouse and sweater? You have scads of clothes, you lucky girl, you. So if I could borrow a skirt for tonight—. . . . Oh def. I got a cute date. . . Certainly you know him. Ken Walker. It'll be a tall evening. A movie first. And then we'll whiz over to the Pink Platter for a snack. And then— . . . Why, Liz. What a nasty crack. Did Ken ever date you? . . . He did . . . Well, get him. So he didn't throw you a crumb. Oh well, I can always have a double order of water. So how about your skirt? . . . Cocoa brown? . . . Sounds terrif. Thanks so much, Liz. I'll be over for it in a jif. . . . My what? . . . No, I'm not using my alligator bag. I'm going to ask Madge for hers. She has a darling yellow one . . . Sure thing. I'll bring it along. Bye, Liz.

Yes, Mother, I know. Just a sec. I must call Elsa and Sue. But Mother, I'm still half undressed—for tonight, I mean.

Hello, Elsa? Is that you? . . . What's crunching? . . . Oh sure. You got a passion for carrots. Well, you can be a honey bunny and let me wear that yellow sweater of yours. . . . For tonight. It'll be seen at the best places. . . . Oh, Elsa. You can't do this to me. How could you loan it to Carol. It won't look half as cute on her. When I gave you my saddle shoes you promised that I—. . . . Your deep purple? That would look weird with lemon and cocoa. . . . What? Pale pink and a grey skirt sounds delish. I'll be right over. . . . Oh, Elsa, you're a meanie! A fine time to send them to the cleaners.

Grey and pink. That has real zing. Who could I call? I got it. Donna Lovelace. She has a kick for pink. I'll give her a buzz pronto. Thanks Elsa, for nothing. Bye.

Mother, please. Don't you care about my social life? It will be absolutely ruined unless I call Donna right this second.

Now let's see. Donna has the pink blouse and sweater—I hope. Then I must call back Liz and swap the cocoa skirt for grey. I imagine Madge has another bag. If not, I could try Linda Green.

It's all for a movie date, Mother, with Ken Walker. I was all hep about it until I spoke to the girls. Now I wonder. Will it be a bang or a blister?

MR. RAY OF SUNSHINE

The man of the house breezes down to breakfast to greet his family of three. His voice rings out blithely as he exhibits a smile. All eyes are fixed on him as if they were witnessing a strange attraction.

Good morning, everyone. Claire dear—my little sweetheart, Joan—and Billy boy. Well! All quiet, huh? How about getting a good morning in return? Thank you, thank you, thank you.

Don't we look bright and eager this morning. That's the idea. Start the day with a shine—and it'll shine right back at you.

How nice you look this morning, Claire. You know, I think you look loveliest in the morning. No make-up —hair sort of careless. It gives you that—well—that simple look. And don't glare, honey. That's supposed to be a compliment.

Hey, why doesn't anyone eat—instead of just staring? Mustn't let that good oatmeal get cold, kiddies.

No, thank you, Claire, I don't want to read the newspaper. Let's just have our breakfast served with sparkling conversation. You know, that's the trouble with modern living—not enough time for talk. Too

5

many substitutes—like reading, the movies, television. People aren't talking enough—and before you know it, repressions set in. Then you see a psychiatrist and—

What, dear? Certainly, Claire, I feel fine. Why do you—

Oops! Nothing, dear. Just a shot of grapefruit in the eye. That's all. Certainly I'm not going to fuss about it. Why be upset over trifles?

Billy, are you in a trance? You've been holding that spoon in mid-air ever since I sat down. Of course I'm not grouchy—and don't look so surprised. Your dad has a sunny side to his disposition, too, I want you to know. Yes, I know. I did bawl you out last night. Sorry. But your dad almost took a nose dive down those stairs. Hereafter you'll remember to put your skates in the closet, won't you?

Now Claire dear, if you will, I'll have my eggs. Oh, that's all right. I don't mind if they are a little cold. They probably have more vitamins that way. But honey, I'm not being sarcastic. So don't give me that funny look.

And eat, everyone, for goodness sake. Can't a fellow be chipper without making excuses for it? From the stares I'm getting you'd think I was saying all the wrong answers.

Hmm? What brought all this on? Okay, Claire, I'll tell you. That book—*How to be Happy for Life.* I read a chapter last night. All you do is memorize a few lines every day—and bingo—you're happy for keeps. Just like that.

Joan, my little sugar plum, we don't sing at the table. Hmm? Okay, so you're happy. Drink your milk and we'll all be happy. A happy breakfast is the prelude to a happy day. That's what it says in the book. So—

Hey there. Easy does it, Billy. You got a mouthful of oatmeal and words. Swallow and then— Well, sonny boy, what if it does look like rain? Oh, the Brave Baboons are playing ball this afternoon. Well, you're not going to let that get you down. As it says in the first chapter—be the sun yourself if it isn't up there shining. It's like a boomerang. You get what you give. Make the other fellow happy and you'll get that way yourself. So you see, Billy, if—

Now wait a minute, Claire. Don't scream at the child. Sure, I saw what he did.

Billy boy, you didn't mean to drop the egg all over the table cloth, now did you? Of course you didn't.

Come on, Claire. Look at the sunny side. He could have dropped it on the carpet. That would've been a darn sight worse. So instead of that sharp word, say the first nursery rhyme that comes into your head. Certainly, that's what the book says. Go on, Claire, say it. Well, I never heard that one in *Mother Goose*.

Billy, say I'm sorry to Mother. Because it's good manners, that's why. Thataboy.

What, sweetheart? Yes, Joan, that's what your

daddy said. He's going to do things for people. And we should all try to do the same. What's that? Oh, you still want to take tap dancing lessons, do you? Look, my pet, we discussed that last week and— Huh? Okay, if it'll make you happy, I guess so. Now finish your breakfast.

Golly, look at that view. Bet no one noticed that magnolia tree was blooming. We don't see the beauty around us. We are blind to the common, everyday surroundings. We take too many things for granted and—

What, Claire? Certainly I've looked at the wall paper in the living room lately. What's the matter with it? You don't say. It looked fine to me. Why, it was just papered a couple of years ago. Certainly, dear, I want you to be happy. Okay, okay, we'll see.

Yes, dear, I'll have another cup of coffee. That's another simple pleasure we take for granted. Just gulp and run.

Say something, Billy? Come on, speak up. Oh. You want to be a drummer. And how much will it cost? Wow. $129.95 for a pile of noise. There's enough racket going on in this house without paying for more. Uh huh, I see. It'll make you happy. Look, Billy boy, couldn't you be just as happy playing the harmonica? Think how easy it'll be to carry around. Just drop it in your pocket and you're all set for a concert.

Yes, Claire, so I see. Quite a stack of mail. Mostly bills, I imagine, this being the second of the month.

Ah, not at all, Claire. I don't mind a bit. Of course, shopping makes you happy.

This one's from Pritchard's. Let's open it and know the worst. One Tropical Temptation $3.59. Translate that, will you, dear? Oh, sun tan oil. A sunburn would be a lot cheaper. No, Claire, I'm not complaining. One house coat $14.94. One griddle $7.98. Dear, haven't we one of those? Oh, girdle. So it is. And one tube shaving cream 39 cents. Nice of you to remember me, dear. Total $26.90.

Here's the gas bill. Well, that shouldn't have any surprises.

What's this one? Oh, a letter for you. From your mother, huh? Really? So she's going away on a trip. That's good. What! She's coming here—for a month! Not if I can help it! If you think I'll put up with her eagle eye watching every—

Billy! Keep that water gun out of your glass of milk.

Joan, will you stop banging on the table? These kids act like hillbillies.

And as for you, Claire, you're going to write your mother and tell her that— Huh? What book? Oh, the devil with being happy. The guy who wrote that never lived with your mother.

Say, what's wrong with this coffee? Well, it tastes different all of a sudden.

Hand me the newspaper. You bet I'm going to read. Go ahead, glare and scream. We may as well get back to normal.

THE SHOW SHOPPER

Two out-of-towners, female and fiftyish, are scampering toward one of the many theatres which have sprouted up from the asphalt lanes along the West Forties in Manhattan.

Here we are, Clara. This is the theatre. Olympia. Just like the name of the candy store back home on Hill Street. You know, the one run by that Greek family. See, there's the sign—*Strange Enchantment.*

Heavens, look at that long line. And we thought by getting here early we'd avoid the rush. Let's hurry, Clara, before anyone else gets ahead of us.

Hmm? I don't remember. As I was leaving the room, you went back to wash your hands. So I— Oh, for goodness sake, Clara, don't worry about it. Anyway, the hotel pays the electric bill, so don't let it bother you. Tomorrow, when we're home again, is time enough to think about turning off this and that.

Oh dear, I can still taste that flat coffee. Heated over from last week, I wouldn't be surprised. Wish now I'd taken tea, like you. And those eggs were never done three and a half minutes—and the toast absolutely limp. And that waitress. It took forever until she looked at us. And after she did serve us, I had just put down my fork when she snatched away my plate. But we fixed her. I don't tip for bad manners.

You feel all right, Clara? That's good. I have some soda mint tablets in my purse if you reed them. Those griddle cakes you had looked awfully soggy to me. And you with your squeamish stomach.

You know, Clara, I wonder what your Calvin and my Roland would say if we'd set a breakfast like that in front of them? You're absolutely right. We're not appreciated. From morning till night it's cook this, wash out that, mend something else. We might as well be an automaton for all the thanks we get. But I've made a new rule, Clara, and you should do the same. Whenever I want a little relaxation I simply take it. So I look at my television programs, read my Book of the Month, play bridge with the girls every Thursday after—

Say Clara, doesn't that look like Maggie Bascom over there? By the door, in that grey suit with the candy striped blouse, and the turned up nose. No, I guess it isn't. Maggie hasn't such smart clothes. Then too, there's more of Maggie across the hips. Heavens no! She doesn't speak to me either. Ever since she won a waffle iron on that quiz show she hasn't even looked at me.

Goodness, this line doesn't move at all. No wonder. That woman hasn't budged from that ticket window since we've been here. You said it, Clara. The way some people fuss over a theatre ticket.

Oh yes, everyone seems to like this show. That is, all but Fanny Winkler. I met her last week at the market. She was buying some shad and I wanted some tongue so we talked. Well, you know Fanny, how she puts on. She thought the show "too dreary for words—the music too trite—and the ballet too—" something-or-other.

I do too. I think the music is very catchy. The other morning while baking a pineapple turnover I heard *Every Night I Daydream.*

You haven't a radio in your kitchen, have you? Clara, you should. My work skims along so fast and easy, you have no idea. First thing in the morning I have *News and Melody* with my cereal and coffee. While getting lunch I have *Stepmother by Choice,* and *It Could Happen to You.* Then Roland comes home. He just likes to eat, so the radio is off. But while stacking up the dishes I have *The Sorrows of Hilda Sackett,* and *The Other Mrs. Lester* over the dishpan.

At last we're moving a few inches. It's about time.

Where, Clara? Oh yes, aren't they attractive pictures? But then those theatrical photographers know all the good angles—which side of the face is more photogenic—what to do if your nose is too big—how to bring out a chin that's too retiring—and lines and wrinkles they brush out. So there you are. If you and

I had one of those taken, we'd look hon-bun too.

Loretta uses that expression all the time. Someone is either a grim drip or a hon-bun. The language youngsters use these days. Half the time I don't understand her.

Hmm? Yes, I have a little more shopping to do. Some perfume for Loretta. She's always using mine and saying she doesn't. And a polka dot tie for Roland. They're no longer in fashion but that's all he'll ever wear.

Are you getting anything for Calvin? I see. Certainly not. I wouldn't either. If he never brings you a thing when the Happy Beavers have their convention, why should you? That's only a fair exchange.

How many are still ahead of us? You can see the line better than I can. Nine? Well, that shouldn't take too long. I'll get my money ready meanwhile.

We're taking Cousin Thelma and Paul. She's having a birthday again. June twelfth. She's hinted around several times how much she'd like to see this show. And you know Cousin Thelma if she doesn't get her way.

She and Paul took us out to dinner on my birthday. The Purple Pigeon. I'll never forget it. I had a cocktail, broiled lobster, and ptomaine poisoning a little later on. Not that Cousin Thelma could help that, of course. So to return the favor, we'll bring them over here and see a show. As it happens, Roland will have his vacation then so we can drive over. Too bad you can't be with us, Clara. Yes, I know. You're always at the shore at that time.

Hmm? How old she'll be? I can tell you in a minute. Thelma was born after Cousin Harold and before Cousin Minnie. Minnie's four years younger than Harold. Harold is three years older than his sister, Grace. Grace is forty-eight. That makes Harold fifty-one. And he's two years older—so that makes Cousin Thelma forty-nine.

Oh, good, we're almost there now. Listen to him snap at people. Why is it, Clara, that the most impolite man you can find is always behind a ticket window? I don't care if he did hear me. They'd rather bark at you than be polite. Or else pretend they're deaf, all of a sudden—like that bus driver yesterday. Just because I wanted to be sure we were on the right bus was no reason— Oh yes, here we are.

I want four center evenings, first row center, for June twelfth balcony. What? Young man, I told you. I want four balconies for June twelfth center. Now really! I said nothing of the kind.

Clara, perhaps you can make him understand.

Certainly. That's exactly what I said—four balcony seats in the center for June twelfth. What? Nothing until November? But goodness, that's six months away. I might have tonsilitis by then—the theatre might be burned down. Besides it's my Cousin Thelma's birthday and she wouldn't like another in

November. Well, you needn't blast. And you're not a bit sorry.

Come along, Clara. I'm simply boiling. Of all the provoking men he takes the cake—the devil's food. Let's go somewhere and have an ice cream soda.

CEDRIC QUACKENBUSH

An esoteric collection of humans, wearing their brows extremely high, have assembled to hear Cedric Quackenbush, a spellbinder from "across the pond." The sprinkling of applause has subsided, and with British vocal trimmings he launches his tirade.

Thank you, Madame Chairman.

Members of the Valiant Culture Clan, it is indeed a delightful occasion to be here—if I may be the first to say so—and I'm sure the pleasure will be all mine. Rarely have I the privilege of appearing before such an inspiring, alert-looking audience, and this afternoon is no exception.

As your chairman—or rather chairlady—if you don't mind a change of gender in mid-stream—or rather mid-sentence—as she stated so vociferously—in London last year I was presented the Golden Larynx for the best diction heard on public trams by the Academy of Palaver and Persuasion, Limited. I had no sooner finished my acceptance speech when I was requested to leave. You see, as a magnanimous gesture on the part of my countrymen, it was agreed that my gift of oratory should not be confined to

Britannia alone. Jolly old England would have to jolly well do without me.

So here I am on your shores as Ambassador of Verbosity, shall I say—and hobnobbing all over your vast country. Or as you say in your colorful vernacular —I am doing places and going things. I say, that sounds a bit odd, doesn't it? I do believe I've reversed my port and starboard—to get nautical for no rhyme or reason. But as I am trying to elucidate, I'm seeing your country vice versa, if you follow me.

Since everything in this highly commercialized age has a label attached to it, after much pro and conning, I've decided to call my lecture *Loquacity and its Relation to Affluency.* Or to put it in the American idiom—*Shoot the Breeze, Bud, You're Loaded.*

Now how, you may ask, can words we utter with our tongue change over into cash in our pocket? That sounds rather as if one must be a contortionist, doesn't it? But rest assured, good people, it can be done without doing anything so rapturous—or I should say, rupturous. But before we have visions of green-backs dancing before our eyes, let us cogitate.

First of all, let us ask ourselves, "Am I voice conscious?" Not me, actually, as I definitely am. But if I may point the finger and reword the question, "Are *you* voice conscious?" I fear many of you listening to me now will have to confess a "no," which means you're not fully conscious at all. There. Are we hanging our heads in shame? But what to do about it?

Sharpen your ears, as a figure of speech, and listen to what babbles forth from your tongue. Does it fall soft and clear upon the ear—or does it jangle out of tune? Think of your voice as a calling card. It tells the world what you are. Are you proud of what it's saying?

Next, dear Clan of Vulture Covers, ask yourself— I say, does something amuse you?

What, Madame Chairman? My word, did I say that? Pardon me, if I dropped a spoonerism. I do it all the time.

Now as we were. Ask yourself, "Have I a round or a flat voice?" Here again *I* am *you,* to thoroughly confuse you. A round one, I hope, is your answer. And just how can we shape our tones so they'll be round —or to make it sound appetizing and all that sort of thing—pear-shaped? Just by merely yawning gives us the open throat. So if you haven't yawned within the last few minutes, let us do so now. Are we ready? A-a-ah! There. That wasn't a bit difficult, was it? And there we have the open, round position. So next time someone catches you in the act of yawning, merely say, "Pardon me, but I was merely tuning my vocals." They may look at you askance, and never invite you to their home again, but if that's the sort of friends they are, you had better get rid of them once and for all.

I understand you have a quaint custom over here of

setting aside a week to do a certain special thing—
like Polish Your Bifocals Week—Be Kind to the
Chipmunk Week—Knit an Argyle Sock Week—and
many others too humorous to mention. Why not try
a Crisp Your Consonant Week and see what happens.

When I said that the other day, one lady in my
audience thought it meant a new cereal. I must say
your breakfasts over here are so audible. It's amazing. They simply must crinkle, crackle, or crunch, or
Junior won't touch the stuff.

But before good speech can be ours, we must know
what to relax and what to control. For instance, your
diaphragm is the control center. And to illustrate, I
am now placing my hand on said diaphragm. Not
physically touching it, of course, since it's padded
from our touch by articles mentionable and unmen-
tionable. All breath control is focused here, while the
tongue, lips and chin should be relaxed. Sounds
simple as Simon, doesn't it? Yet it's extr'ordin'ry how
many of us do it in reverse—relax what we should
control and vice versa. But once you— Now there
was an American expression I wanted to use here—
but it completely escaped me.

But you may ask, and to put it in your idiom—
How can gib glab stretch the dough? Dash it all. Now
how do you say it—glib gab? Righto. But to carry on.
Successful people have round, vibrant voices. So if
you can say, "How now Horatio, is your brown cow

downtown?", you'll be accepted as one. Not a cow, of course, but a candidate for prosperity. Golden speech and a pocket that jingles can be synonymous.

And that, fellow valiants, is as far as I carry on without having a spot of tea. I dropped a subtle hint to your chairlady as soon as I arrived, and she's been brewing ever since. But while I'm sipping I'll be glad to answer any questions. So if anything tantalizes you, speak up, and we'll be tantalized together.

And now if you'll pardon me while I bend— I say! What is that expression? What do you Americans bend while having tea? Oh, thank you. An elbow, of course. How original you Americans are.

And now, Madame Chairman, may I tip a sip to the lip?

MRS. WINTHROP REQUESTS

A modishly gowned woman, with a Martini as companion, steps out upon the veranda of a fashionable residence on Long Island. She glances about, then turns to leave the shadowed retreat, when she notices the silhouette of a feminine form nearby.

Oh. Pardon me. I didn't see you at first. The lighting out here is meant to be only incidental. How odd —the veranda so deserted for the moment. This is usually the most tempting hide-away—after a round or two at the bar.

But you, my dear, are far too attractive to be here alone. And not even a cocktail to keep you company.

Strenuous party in there, isn't it? I can endure it for just so long and then I crave a Martini in solitude. But then, it's the sort of party society columns play up as *brilliant, gala,* or some such superlative. All you need is some fashionable music—it's Mexican tonight —and a line-up of drinks.

Are you having a good time? Neither am I—although it's my party. Oh yes, I'm Mrs. Winthrop. Didn't you know? Oh, that's all right. Don't be sorry. Whenever herds of people are invited there're always a few extras crashing in. It's flattering in a way. A guarantee that one's parties are successful, or why would they bother?

But then all of this is my husband's doing. You know Jeffrey, of course? Now don't be demure, my dear. I'm sure you do. Though it would be a novelty if you didn't. In case you haven't heard, Jeffrey was an actor—and had a long reign as a matinee idol. To flatter his ego he still pretends he'll make a comeback. So every so often he must throw a party for "professional contacts," he calls it, when up pops a flock of lovely women. Jeffrey, of course, fancies himself the irresistible decoy. Every woman here has some design on him—so Jeffrey would like to believe. So you see, my dear, it's a game of keen competition. A survival of the fairest.

You look surprised. I'm just being horribly candid. I don't mind telling you that I've given up bidding. I'm what is prosaically labelled—"the neglected wife."

Oh, please don't leave. I can't bear to be alone just yet. I don't know why I'm prattling away like this. I wasn't up to it in there. Afraid I know some of them too well. Conversation was becoming more deadly by the minute. At least I can be frank with you, because we're absolute strangers.

But I would love another Martini. Henry should be along shortly. A remarkable houseboy, Henry. He knows instinctively when I'm ready for another.

How disgusting. I'm out of cigarettes. Oh, you have. Thank you, my dear. I have a lighter. Yes, it is a rather attractive case. It's mother-of-pearl—with my initials in gold. The only one like it in Paris. Jeffrey bought it for me on our honeymoon.

He was most attentive—as the ardent beau. He'd remember all those special touches—my favorite perfume—a camellia or two for a new dress—to whisper pretty nothings in my ear. That was our honeymoon —the first act—but it had a quick curtain.

What, dear? Oh, I'm glad you like our home. I suppose it's like many a Long Island estate. House in English Tudor, stone-flagged terrace, formal garden, a yacht or two. It can all be pretty dismal when you're alone. When days and even weeks go by while Jeffrey is away playing the debonair lover. But forgive me. I seem to be babbling about Jeffrey all the time.

What's the matter, dear? You seem so uneasy all of a sudden. Have I said something that— But of course. I should have known. You're out here to meet someone. I'm afraid he's late, isn't he? He surely couldn't forget about you, now could he?

Who's there? Oh, it's you, Henry. I'm over here— and famished for one of those. Thank you, Henry. Perhaps the young lady would like another.

Do, my dear. Something tells me you're going to need it.

That'll be all, Henry.

Afraid I lost count on these. All that matters is that things seem so—so trivial—delightfully trivial—after a number of them. I can even pretend to be blasé about Jeffrey. As if one more love affair didn't matter.

But where is your young man? Or perhaps he isn't so young? Please, my dear, don't overdo the modesty trick. I know you are waiting for Jeffrey. Very well, since you're acting so naïve, suppose I tell you that I was in the lounge too—at that moment. You remember an hour or so ago—when Jeffrey was showing off his trophies. Oh, don't look embarrassed. I didn't hear a word. But I understood his look. Having seen Jeffrey in all his plays, I know every nuance of expression. He loves nothing better than to play a love scene on the slightest cue.

Well, at last you're admitting it. No, I shan't ask questions. I'm not curious about how or where you met him. But since we're playing the truth game, I don't mind telling you I'm jealous. I loathe these parties, when all they mean are chances for Jeffrey to flirt. Deep down I'm still hopelessly in love. Quaint of me, isn't it, when I know every one of Jeffrey's bagful of tricks! He charmed me into believing it was all for love. All too soon I knew it was only because I could pick up the check. Jeffrey is expensive to keep. He's become a luxury that I can't give up.

But there. This will never do. I'm becoming lush. I'm afraid you're seeing me as the wilted wife—and I don't like it.

Let's go inside. Perhaps some of that Mexican music will revive us. We'll have Louis mix us another. But wait a moment, dear, while I put on some lipstick. This is my party—so I must put on my jolliest party face.

DOORSTEP SALESMAN

Every spring, along with the weed, the wasp, and other outdoor pests, a variety of door-to-door salesmen sprout up. One of these hardy perennials of the book-selling species, glowing with enthusiasm for his product, greets "the lady of the house," who happens to be, in this instance, a frowzy female of visible disinterest.

Good morning, madam. I thought for a minute you weren't home. But I heard a baby crying somewhere, and the radio going, so I just rang on. Oh, I understand. It's one of those mornings when everything annoying turns up. But I'll take just a minute of your time.

Now just a moment, madam. Before you say you don't want to buy anything, may I ask you a question? No? Well, I will anyway. When you're out socially, wouldn't you like to be the center of attraction? You wouldn't? Now madam, you surely don't want to neglect your I.Q. You have a bottle of those? I'm afraid you don't understand. I'm not talking about vitamins.

No, madam, I'm not selling insurance. I just happen to represent the most instructive book you ever put on a shelf. It's called *You're Smarter Then You Think.*

Yes, yes, I know. You have too many books already. Most housewives say that—or else that they'd rather look at television than read. But with our method you can watch television and yet have time to improve the mind, too. You simply follow our page-a-day plan, and before—

Oh, I see. You fall asleep when you read. Well, madam, I can assure you that won't happen when reading this book. No indeed. It's big and heavy, you see. 1,311 pages. If you drop it on your lap, it'll wake you up.

Oh, don't go away, madam. That's all right. If something's burning on the stove I'll come along to the kitchen. I can sell a book anywhere. The other day I made a sale in a cemetery.

I see. It's time for the baby's lunch. How about trying something different? All you have to do is open the book to the chapter on Recipes—Junior Size.

Hello. Here's the baby now. What's her name? Althea. And do you know what it means? Certainly, it's a girl's name—but Althea has a special meaning all its own. To find out, all we do is open the book and look under A for Althea. Here we are—adenoids —alley cat—Althea. "Proper feminine name derived from the Greek; given the power of healing." There you are. Althea should become a fine nurse when she grows up. Oh, you want her to be a waitress. Well, she can take the temperature of a baked potato.

Look, madam, before you close the door on my toe, let me read the names of the ladies here in your block who are buying this book. For instance, there's Mrs. White. You know her, I suppose? Oh, I see. She's on the same telephone line. Then I'm sure you're well acquainted. She bought two books. One for her boy in college—just in case the juke box broke down. And another for a wedding gift to a cousin in Nebraska. It seems that her cousin sent her a set of Dickens which she never read—and now she wants to do the same for her cousin.

Then Mrs. Cunningham across the street. She liked the "intellectual tone," as she called it, the book gave to her Chippendale table. Then Mrs. Lewis next door. She's a widow, I believe, and wants something heavy around just in case of burglars. So she bought one to read in bed.

What? Yes, I see. The baby wants the book. Oh, not at all. Let her touch it. The cover is a dirty brown. We think of everything.

So you see, madam, all the different ways this book can be of service. Surely you want to be as smart as the other women in your neighborhood. Oh. Well, even if you are moving away next month, you still should—

What, madam? Certainly. This volume can give

every kind of information. Can it do what? Well, that is an unusual request—but I suppose it could keep your husband home at night. Now let's see.

How about letting him count the punctuation marks on a page. Make a game out of it. For every comma score 1 point—every period 2—and so on. Each time he scores a hundred you might give him a kiss. He'll either become so drowsy that he'll fall asleep—or else he'll want to neck instead. There. Doesn't that sound like fun?

Just a minute, madam, before you shut— Ow! That isn't my spare foot. Don't worry, ma'am, I won't be back. One more like you and I'll peddle boxing gloves.

SHOW GIRL

The music has swelled its last brassy chord—the flashy finale is over—and so is zippered up, in the wee hours of the morn, the last floor show at the Lucky Eleven Club. It is one of the tawdry night spots found along a narrow street in "the Village."

Up in the dressing room, a flock of girls are in all stages of dress and undress. One of them, a sleek blonde by her own choice, joins in the free-for-all gab jive.

Well, kids, we can wrap up the torso until tomorrow. An' who's sorry? I'm beat. After doin' three of these a night, why didn't I take up shorthand?

Yeah, Carol, I caught your new routine. What do ya call it? The Spirit of the Sea Foam. Mm, sorta fa-de-la. Oh, I get it. Interpretative stuff. I suppose that wisp of chiffon ya wear is the splash. An' the old bump an' grind are the heavin' of the waves. Right? Sure, call it art. That's us all over.

Say, any of you gorgeous hags see my comb? It was here a— Well, toss it over, Sandra, will ya? How we girls share. If anyone broke out with anythin' contagious it'd be just too bad.

Hey, cover it up, girls. Hank's in again. He might at least go through the motions of knockin'. Just because he's doorman he thinks our dressing room is an open invitation. Certainly. I still got my blush of modesty.

Talkin' to me, Hank? Ya don't say. Someone to see me, huh? Okay, Hank, tell him to wait. Huh? A young lady? Now ya got me guessin'. I don't know any. Send her up.

Yeah, Polly, I'm almost ready. Are we gonna feed the face? I could go for a bowl of soup, an' somethin' on rye, an'—

Who's knockin'? Oh, yeh. I almost forgot. My public. Come in!

Oh. Hello there, honey. Ya—ya want to see me? Why no, I'm sorry. I don't seem to know ya. Amy Thomas? Hi. That's right. Taffy Sweet is what they call me on the billing. Sure it's phoney. I'm Gertie Murray for real.

Now how about that. So ya thought I'd be Vera Wendling. Where from? Dixon, Iowa. The corn country, huh? Sorry, honey. I'm strictly from Jersey.

Oh, that's all right, Amy. Glad ya stopped by. Catch our show? Uh huh. Now don't tell me ya just walked by—saw my picture outside—an' thought of Vera Wangle-dangle? Well, now that ya got a close look, guess ya know. Be good to yourself, Amy. So long.

Huh? Yeah, she was cute. Go on, girls, scram. I

gotta fix the face. I'll see ya over a sandwich. Save a place for me.

Go ahead, Polly. Ya needn't wait around for me. Yeah. That's exactly what I'm in—a daze.

Polly, if I let you in on a secret—ya won't blab it to the others? Go ahead an' take a good look at Vera Wendling. The same. An' from Iowa yet. I feel like a crumb to let Amy go away like that. But up she pops—all the girls have ears on—so I didn't go along with it.

Yeah, we lived in the same town. Population 226. An' the kids did call me Taffy. I never knew why. We had those girly, pretty pink dreams. Amy was going to be a librarian. An' for me, the ballerina—only I made it in burly instead. But if I know Amy, she's the best librarian in the biz.

It's about six years since I left Dixon. I never kept in touch with Amy. Kickin' it up in these rat holes isn't the thing you'd write on a post card. Even my folks don't know. They think I'm a hostess at Schrafft's. An' there's the story of my life.

Just a dab of perfume, Polly, an' I'll be with ya. Guess Amy didn't need a second glance to see this couldn't happen to Vera. It isn't just the blonde bleach that's different. Vera didn't have the same down beat. Know what I mean?

Okay, Polly, so ya rather eat than think. I'm put together. Let's go. Oh, here's Hank again. Guess he wants to lock up.

Keep your teeth in, Hank. We're leavin'. Huh? A note for me? Thanks.

Yeah, it's from Amy. Listen to this. "You didn't fool me, Vera. I understand why you pretended. I'm having coffee across the street. Please join me. Amy."

Get that, Polly? She knew all the time. It means Vera Wendling still shows. An' do I like it! It's a bigger bang than—than gettin' an orchid.

See ya later, Polly. I want to hear all about Iowa —talk Iowa—an' smell Iowa. From now on ya can call me Taffy Cornball an' I'll love it.

FOURSCORE AND TEN

A large portion of summertime in a small town can be spent on the front porch. Coming out for a morning sit is Jonathan Obediah Thompkins, a spry specimen of ninety. Wiping away the remnants of breakfast from bearded lips, he spies his daughter, Lucy, who is busy tidying up.

Good mornin', Lucy. No indeedy, I ain't up early. The days are short enough—so why go an' sleep 'em away. Huh? Yep, I had my breakfast. Went an' helped myself. Now Lucy, stop treatin' me like a—a relic. I ain't gonna fall to pieces because I heated up some oatmeal an' poured myself a cup of coffee.

Yep, I got the mornin' paper. So don't bother about me. Keep right on dustin' or whatever you're doin'.

What, Lucy? Sure I know what day it is. Friday. Shucks yes, I know. It's my birthday. Thank ya, Lucy. It will be a happy one if ya jest forget about it. My, them flies is pesty this mornin'. Shoo!

Hmm? Sure, I'm wearin' my old suit. Why not? Now Lucy, why should I wear my Sunday best jest because it's my birthday. It's like any other day to me. Anyhow, that there Sunday suit must last a good

long time. I'm gonna be buried in it. So why should
I dress up fer my funeral today? Heh, heh. I was
jest teasin' ya, Lucy.

Hmm? The mornin' mail? No, I ain't seen it yet.
Why? Well, I'll be— Twenty-three birthday cards, ya
say. Folks shouldn't go to all that trouble. Betcha
they say every year, "This is the last one we have to
send that old buffalo,"—but I fool 'em.

Where in blazes is the funny page? Huh? No, Lucy,
don't bring 'em out now. I'll look 'em over later on.

Who are ya talkin' to, Lucy? Martha Williams?

Oh, good mornin', Martha. Catchin' the bus to the
city? Better get a wiggle on.

Well, Lucy, I'm glad you two got over yer spat.
That was a darn fool thing to get into a huff about.
Jest because ya both grabbed the same dress at that
rummage sale.

Why all the fuss an' bother? The porch is in apple
pie order. That dustin' won't do a speck of good until
we get some rain. Huh? We're gettin' company?
Who? Now why in thunderation does a newspaper
man went to see me?

An interview, huh? An' jest because I'm ninety
years old. By golly, ya'd think I was the oldest
scalawag in captivity. Well, he won't ketch me. Not
if I see him first.

Lucy, what are ya jabberin' about—us bein' the
first family? Anyone knows that Adam an' Eve was—
Oh, is that what ya mean? Yep, yer great grandpa an'

his family was the first settlers in this here town. But
that ain't news. You've been braggin' about that ever
since ya wore pigtails. So—

Huh? Oh, good mornin', Ben. What? Ya don't say!
It jest come in, huh? Do I want to see it. Jest try an'
keep me away.

Now Lucy, it's jest around the corner. It ain't every
day a new fire engine comes to town. So why—

Oh, look there. A car jest pulled up. If it's that
newspaper feller, jest tell him I ain't here. Tell him I
went to jail. Tell him anythin' only— Lucy, if you
think I'm gonna tell my obituary to— Huh? Oh
shucks. Here he is.

Good mornin', young feller. Nice of ya to stop by,
but I was jest about to—

Go on awhile, Ben. See ya there. I got roped in on
somethin' here.

Yes, sir. Lucy, my daughter here, told me. An' I
don't mind tellin' ya that I tried to wriggle out of
this. Uh huh. So ya want one of them interviews an'
a pitcher, do ya? Well, afraid ya'll stay awhile, so ya
may as well set.

What's that? Oh, ya want to take it now. Go ahead.
Guess I'm as ready now as I'll ever be.

Let me alone, Lucy. My hair's all right. If it wasn't
mussed up I wouldn't look natural. Now stop fussin'.
The dandruff won't show. Jest set over there, Lucy,
an' watch the birdie—like we used to say. Oh, darn.

A fly is tryin' to land on my nose. Shoo! Yep, go ahead. Yes, Lucy, I'm smilin'.

Well, thank goodness that's over. Better look if it didn't crack the camera. Now that I've been snapped, if you'll excuse me, I got to— Huh? Oh, yes, the blame interview. Fire away.

My full name is Jonathan Obediah Thompkins. They called me Spif—when I was a young whipper-snapper. Yessiree, I've been livin' here in Springtown all my life. But I'm still—how do they say it—right on the beam. Yessiree.

Yep, that's right. My grandpa, Ezra Thompkins, he come here to Springtown—only it wasn't called nothin' then—an' put up the first house. Shucks, I plum forgot what year it was. Ask Lucy. She rattles off all them dates like a history book. Yep, guess that's right. 1842.

Yes, indeedy. This town sure has changed. Why I can remember the time there was only five houses here. An' would ya believe it, our post office was a livery stable in them days—with horseflies buzzin' around instead of busybodies. An' the nearest store —eighteen miles away. We'd hitch up Bessie an' drive over every Saturday evenin'.

What ya say? Got any hobbies? Ya betcha I have. Every afternoon Ben Roberts comes by an' we have a game of pinochle. Checkers? I should say not! That's too old fogey. Then I watch television—if it

ain't one of them sticky love stories. I like them murder ones best. Saw a humdinger last night. Eight
people was done away with before they spoke about
hair tonic.

How's that again? If I prefer the good old days to
these, huh? No indeedy. All these modern contrap-
tions suit me—okey-doke. Been up in one of them
airplanes a couple of times. Now I'm itchin' to go up
all the way an' see how they gad around on the moon.
With all them new fangled inventions comin' along
—well, I'm jest too blame nosey. I want to see 'em
all an' try 'em all.

Say, ya sure got a lot down there on that paper.
Guess ya got enough, huh? That's good. Oh, guess I
have to say yer welcome. It'll be in tomorrow's paper,
huh? I sure will read it. An' that pitcher better be
good too—or I won't so much as look at yer blame
paper again—'cept fer Li'l Abner.

Well, goodbye, young feller. I'll let ya come around
again—when I hit a hundred.

Thank goodness that's over. Gosh darn, if I don't
feel ready for a crepe. Well, I gotto do somethin'
about that. Hmm? Well, Lucy, I'll tell ya. I'm goin'
in an' take my vitamin pill—an' then get a look at
that fire engine. That's what I'll do.

LADY OF THE MORNING

A fluffy she, of a questionable fifty, is prettily ar-
ranged behind a table in a television studio. It is just
a minute before air time, and the lady gives a final
pat to hat, hair, and corsage.

Tell me when, Mr. Valentine. This is my first television appearance, you know, and I'm somewhat
a-twitter. I hope the camera gets my best angles.
What? Yes, I'll watch for the red light. Now?

Happy morning, ladies. This is Drusilla Hooker,
your Lady of the Morning.

Well, here I am in a new dimension. You're all so
well acquainted with my voice, you dear, loyal
friends of my radio program. But one must forsake
the old for the new. So here's the same voice and the
package that comes with it.

Now ladies, are you ready to let that mop and dust
cloth fall where they may? Fine. Pull up a chair, my
dear, and lend a pretty ear.

We have so many exciting topics to discuss. There's
a fashion hint I want to pass along. I must tell you
all about a buffet supper I attended last evening.
Then a recipe that will make your tongue tingle with

anticipation. And some choice tidbits from our "Have You Heard" department.

It's a perfectly gorgeous morning here in New York. Lady Springtime has finally arrived and she's having a gay time splashing about her profusion of colors.

Which reminds me that Jiffy Glow Enamel is available in such a large variety of colors that Dame Nature herself could turn pale with envy. Remember our little jingle:

> Spatter, spatter as you go,
> When the enamel is Jiffy Glow!

How am I coming in, ladies? Or I should say—how is my video? To use television terms. Perhaps a little more profile would be nice. Camera man, would you be so kind as to— Isn't that cute. He's waving at me. Well, on we go—photogenic or not.

On a radiant morning like this, one should have that—well, the French thought of it first—that *joie de vivre* sort of feeling. If you're not filled with *joie* —or for that matter *vivre*—could it be that you didn't have a glass of Goldie orange juice for breakfast? Remember ladies:

> For zip and go—or go and zip—
> It's Goldie Orange Juice you'll sip!

And now for our first "Have-You-Heard." It's about Dolores Linden, who is called in the Hollywood vernacular, "The Gasp." How we sighed with envy over that satiny complexion of hers. Well, it's been reported from those in the know, that upon each damask cheek is a generous coating of freckles. Yes, that's what I said—freckles. But how does Miss Linden play such a bewitching deceiver? By using an amazing liquid make-up called "Peek-a-Boo." So all you have to do, ladies, is to go to your druggist and say "Peek-a-Boo."

Here's a thrilling "Have-You-Heard." Joel Morley, your favorite man of brawn and charm, has broken free from the fetters of matrimony. So again we can place him on our list of eligible males. Remember last fall when I conducted a poll to find out which man you'd like to share a triple-decker sandwich with —and your unanimous choice was Joel Morley? Well, I must confess, he was my candidate too. And no wonder, with that captivating smile of his. He uses Perlatine, of course. So everytime you're standing in front of your mirror, brushing your teeth with Perlatine, say to yourselves, "Perhaps Joel Morley is doing the very same thing right now." And sure enough, with a little imagination, there he'll be smiling back at you. Can you think of a more tantalizing inducement? So Perlatine away, ladies.

Oh, here comes the camera for a close-up. A dolly

shot, they call it. Perhaps we should all smile in unison, shall we? There.

Now then, where were we? Oh yes, our question-and-answer session.

In the mail the other day, I received an urgent inquiry from a Mrs. Murray of Shaker Heights. She was in a dither as to whether the nail polish should match when she's having a manicure and a pedicure. Yes, Mrs. Murray, I think the same shade should do the double glamour job. So these sunny mornings, when our little pinkies peep through our play shoes, it is so chic to have, say, Riot Red, on fingers and toes. That's just one of the many flattering shades put up by Razzle Dazzle.

Right here I'm supposed to stretch out my hands for a close-up. You see, ladies, I can now demonstrate the products I recommend. Intriguing, isn't it? Always remember:

> If it's males you wish to dazzle,
> It's Razzle Dazzle for your nails.

And now to tell you about a really sumptuous affair that took place last evening. It was a buffet party given to launch the Society to Perpetuate the Turtle in this country. It was held in the Diaphanous Room in the Hotel Regal. Lady Broccoli—looking exactly like the vegetable—I mean, the spelling of it—but emphasis on the second syllable—Lady Broccoli—

was the guest of honor. It seems she started a similar movement in London some years ago. She looked most picturesque in delphinium taffeta with the skirt billowing out in a commotion of ruffles.

But to dwell a bit on the lowly turtle for a moment. The male, it seems, can express a variety of sounds from a piping squeak to a hoarse bellow—while the sad little female can only reply with a hiss. Now I ask you, is that being fair to the fair sex?

Just listening to these fascinating facts, I became intrigued with the idea of adopting a pair. Now that I've passed on this lovely thought, I know many of you ladies will do the same. Do send for my booklet —*Get Maternal About the Turtle.*

But enough of the tinsel of night life. Let us get ginghamy and kitchennettish as I read off a tempting recipe called "Coconut Fluff." In case you haven't a pencil and paper at your elbow, I'll dally a moment while you dash for them.

Here is the time I wish I could play a little piano interlude. A waltz by Strauss would be lovely right now, wouldn't it? In fact, kitchen drudgery can become a frolic when doing it with music in three-quarter time. Of course we can't put a piano in the kitchen. But if we're the wise wifey, we do see to it that a portable radio is close to our pots and pans. And if you haven't guessed the name, I mean Minstat —an abbreviation for minus static. Only the Minstat radio offers you sets in four colors especially suitable for the kitchen. They are tomato red, string bean yellow, spinach green, and oyster-shell white.

Now, ladies, have you paper and pencil in hand? Good.

The chief ingredient in our Coconut Fluff is, of course, coconut. Any which kind of brand? Goodness no. Nothing but Creamy Crunch on the label. And by merely adding this and that, you've never seen coconut so altered. Now just jot this down. We take one teaspoon—

What? Oh, no, we can't be! Mr. Valentine, do you mean we're off the air? How dreadful. I ran overtime? Really, Mr. Valentine, in my twelve years on radio not once was I snipped off before I said *au revoir* to the ladies. This is most distressing. To think that I, Drusilla Hooker, was dissolved in the middle of a syllable. Have you an aspirin, Mr. Valentine? I feel ready for another commercial.

SAILOR, BEHAVE

*Two sailors are ambling along one of the paved
lanes in Central Park. One of them, with a southern
drawl, is giving out on his favorite subject—women.*

Well, here's the park, the bench, an' two gobs
plenty willin'—but where're the dames? Look, Steve,
are you sure you're to meet her right here—by the
duck pond? Uh huh. Sure, I called up Gladys an' told
her to be here by four. Yeah, it's ten after. Well, at
least the ducks showed up. Let's take a lease on this
bench an' see what gives.

You know, Steve, I ain't too keen about these
double dates. You all gotta be mighty willin' to do
the same thing—or else it's a floppo. Oh sure, we can
give it a try.

Suppose we check the treasury. I got all of two
bucks an' a buffalo. How much is holdin' you down?
Three green ones an' thirty cents. Let's see—that's a
grand total of five thirty-five. An' into four shares—
that's around a buck an 'a quarter for each. Wow,
can we have a ball. I hope they had a big lunch.

Well, Steve, what'll we do first? We better start
with somethin' for free. The zoo? Dandy. There's

45

nothin' like the zoo to get better acquainted. An' then—

Huh? Naw, that ain't Gladys. She's more whistle bait. Last night she was wearin' a red dress with hair to match. Huh uh, that's the real color. At least she's been a redhead since Saturday. That's when I learned to say Gladys. Huh? Who cares about last names. I got her phone number.

How about a quickie on yours? You just met her last night, huh? What's she like? Uh huh. Chalk up another blonde. What's her name? Cookie. Say, I thought you met a Cookie the other night? Oh. This week you call 'em all Cookie. What'll they be next week—Cup Cake?

Hey, where are you goin'? Okay, take a quick cruise. But don't navigate too far—or Cookie may sugar talk another guy.

Huh? Sorry, Buster. No shine today. Try me tomorrow.

Hello there. Excuse me, honey, for speakin' up, but you're sittin' on— I mean, are you lookin' for a sailor? Great. We're to meet here—where the ducks go quack quack—an' you bein' blonde an' all—you must be Cookie.

I'm Bob. Steve went that way to look for you. An' I'm waitin' around for my sugar lump, Gladys. So I'll share this bench with you until—

Reckon you're right, ma'am. I'm from the south. Atlanta. My drawl kinda gives it away. Oh, you're

from the south too? Sure 'nuff? Where? South Orange.
I have to look that one up.

Right you are, honey. We southerners can get
mighty friendly on short notice. An' if I may say so,
you're no orange ice yourself. I mean, must you put
your arms around me? Not that I—but if Steve should
come along an' see us in a squeeze like this— Sure,
honey, I go for you too, but I have some of that on
order. Gladys. She'll bounce by any minute.

Hey, there's Steve now. Well, hush my gapin'
mouth! He won another doll. Wow! Is he in a spot?
With two Cookies on the string, which one will be
the ginger snap?

Hi, chum. What game are you playin'? Here I have
one Cookie on the fire, while you got— A redhead.
Gladys!

Well, Gladys, explain away, if you can. You an' me
had a date at four. At quarter past you're doin' a
fandango with Steve.

Huh? Not a bit. You got that wrong, Gladys. This
here is Cookie. She's for Steve. I was just sittin' by—
waitin' for you.

Go on, man, tell Gladys this piece of pastry is
yours. What! You never saw her before!

Cookie, you remember Steve here. So why don't
you— An' don't call me sugarfoot.

Wow! This is what I call a quick switch. Huh uh,
I don't mind. Go ahead, Steve. Take Gladys an' navigate. It'll be fun to learn more about South Orange.

Right, Cookie? Easy there, baby. Give me a smoke signal before you kiss.

Looks like a large evenin' ahead, girls. Steve fixed up a tour at the zoo. An' after that, how about a slow boat to Staten Island? Come on, crew, let's paddle.

MINERVA DINGLE

*The neatly painted sign, Old Hickory Lunch Room,
glistens invitingly along the rain-spattered highway.
Inside the green-and-white frame house sits Minerva
Dingle in a rocker by the lace-curtained window.
Even though her hair has turned grey and she no
longer mentions her age, her fingers have lost none
of their nimbleness, as she handles her crochet needle.
The rocking and the busy fingers stop suddenly, as
she hears a car drive up. A moment later the door of
the lunch room opens.*

Oh, good morning, Mister. If ya can call this kinda
weather good. Come right on in. Yes, indeed. It sure
must be nasty fer drivin'. Ever since six o'clock it's
been comin' down somethin' fierce.

Just hang yer hat an' coat up over there an' set
down. Come far from here? Brooktown? Oh my,
that's quite a ways. We ain't been up that way since
—let me see now—guess 'twas the summer we had
our last litter of pigs. So it was. We took 'em up to
one of them county fairs. They gave away a blue
ribbon an' a prize fer the best pigs—an' we got 'em—
Elmer an' me.

49

But mercy, here I am chatterin' away when you're jest droolin 'fer yer breakfast, I imagine. Ya certainly came far on a empty stomach.

Let's see now. I got all kinds of cereal. Now Elmer, he likes oatmeal. Always did. He won't try none of that crispy, crunchy stuff. Every mornin', year in an' year out, there sits Elmer with a oatmeal bowl in front of him. It's gettin' kinda tiresome now—jest to watch him eat it. Then I can fix up some eggs—any way ya like. I always have mine soft boiled. My stomach's sorta finicky. Fried? I certainly can. An' toast an' coffee, ya say.

Why of course ya can. Jest look around as much as ya like. There're all sorts of antiques about. We was ready to throw the stuff out—until people began to make a fuss over it. But talkin' of antiques—that reminds me.

Elmer! Elmer! Ain't ya fixed that chair yet? What? Well, it's high time. An' if ya'd wear yer teeth a body could understand ya.

I declare! That man's been in the cellar putterin' around since breakfast. One of them horsehair chairs tickled too much when ya sat on it. So Elmer had the bright notion he could take out the tickle.

Would ya like some jelly with yer toast? I put up some real good elderberry. Of course ya will.

What ya say? Oh yes, that's an old gramaphone. It was a weddin' present from Elmer's folks. Still play it once in a while—fer old times' sake, I guess. The records sound worn an' scratchy—but so are we.

There—yer eggs are ready. Don't they look perty with their big yeller eyes? Now yer toast. An' a nice hot cup of coffee. The cream an' sugar is right by yer elbow there. Well, I guess the rest of the motions ya can do yerself.

I hope ya don't mind if I set here an' chat with ya. It gets sorta lonesome here sometimes—especially on a day like this. As fer Elmer—he ain't what ya'd call entertainin'. When he putters around he whistles an' when he sets around he jest snoozes. But ya can't make over a husband like ya can a—a pair of window curtains.

Funny how it happened. I never gave Elmer half a look. But that mornin' when he strutted up Main Street, smilin' from ear to ear, an' showin' off them pretty store teeth— Well, we talked that mornin'. An' what did I do but invite him over to play parchesi that evenin'. We got married the next Thanksgivin' Day. Now I sometimes think April Fool day is more suitable fer a weddin'.

How about some more coffee? Of course ya will. What's that? Yes, we're doin' real well here. This little lunch counter is jest enough to keep us from gettin' mouldy. But sometimes I get plain aggravated —to think that I picked out Elmer fer his beautiful teeth—an' now that I have him, he don't wear 'em.

They hurt, he says. His mouth feels like a concrete bridge. Piffles! But whenever company comes an' I see them first, I make him plunk them in.

Oh my. I see ya gobbled up every crumb. I'm glad. That's forty-five cents. Thank ya, Mister.

Must ya be goin' so soon? I see. Yes, that's quite a trip. Yer hat an' coat are all dried off, ain't they? Sure, I'll come along to the door with ya. I want to see if the rain—

Mercy. Still pourin' down. Goodbye, Mister. Watch out fer that pud— Oh dear. Ya stepped right in it. Did it splash ya much? Perhaps it won't show. Goodbye. Come around again' an' meet Elmer. I'll have him smile for ya. Goodbye.

PRODIGAL NEPHEW

*A car skims along the highway past billboard, field
and farm. Sharing the front seat are three occupants
—a family trio—reading from left to right—father,
daughter, and mother. They are nearing the end of
their journey to attend one of those affairs commonly
called a family reunion. The "he" behind the steering
wheel is taking his turn talking away some of the
mileage.*

Just three more miles to go, Millie, then dear
cousins, aunts, and uncles here we come. Huh? Don't
ask me. I lost count. But there'll be a herd of us
Morgans. You can count on that. And what a fuss
they'll make over us—and we'll do the same. Down
the line we'll go. A kiss for every aunt. A handshake
here and a backslap there. Brother, what a workout.

Anyhow, we're doing all this for good old Aunt
Sophie. Every so often she rounds us up. But I have
an idea this'll be the last one. The old girl is hitting
a high score.

What, Caroline? Look—do one thing at a time. Just
talk or just snap bubbles. All right. Now what is it?
I don't know how many little boys and girls will be

there. You'll find someone to fight with, don't worry about that.

Say, doesn't the car look great? Glad I had it washed and simonized. You'd never guess it was a five-year old model. But Cousin Roy will. He sells them. I have my eye on a new Cadillac. And just as soon as we come into some money—

I didn't say that, Millie. Why, I hope Aunt Sophie hits 85 at least. Huh? Oh, she's about 83 now.

Caroline, will you stop squirming? Yes, we'll be there in a few minutes. Then you can run riot, all I care.

What, Millie? Well, that's a fine thing to say. What do you think we are—a pack of animated zombies? It won't be that gruesome. After all, you did meet a few of them here and there.

Caroline, will you quit jabbing me in the eye? Okay, so you love me all of a sudden. But must you get your sticky fingers all over my neck? And throw away that bubble gum. It's been popping since— Hey, not on the floor.

This kid could learn a few manners. Millie, will you do something about her hands? And she could use a comb through that mop.

And that reminds me, young lady. Don't ask Uncle Horace to take off his hair—like you did at Barbara Jane's wedding. Because he wants people to think it's his own, that's why. Uncle Horace has been wearing a toupee for almost twenty years, but he's still sensitive about it.

I suppose the old family tree shook off a few spotty characters. But around Aunt Sophie they gleam good as gold. All they want to know is—who will hit the jackpot when she goes? Downright greedy. Just because she has close to a million, do you think I'm showing up just for a handout?

Millie! Must you be so blunt. Why, I love the old gal. And I rate with her. She always made more fuss over me than Ambrose—or Lillian—or any of 'em.

Say, we didn't forget the peanut brittle, did we? Good. Aunt Sophie has a passion for the stuff.

You know, Millie, I still regret we didn't christen Caroline after her. She would've done all sorts of things for little Sophie that— Yes, honey, I know. It was your dying grandmother's wish—because she lived in South Carolina. I still say that's taking advantage of a Yankee's good nature. Lucky thing she didn't live in Nebraska.

What, sweetie? No, that isn't the name of a cracker. Nebraska is a state—like New Jersey. Huh uh. There's no Atlantic City there. Mosquitoes? I suppose so.

Well, it won't be long now. Just around this hill and we're there. I hope I'll call 'em by their right names. But there'll be changes. Got to expect that. Some will be fatter—others thinner—some getting grey—others bald. Sounds downright depressing.

If I must say it myself, there's no mid-section spread on this ol' boy. Okay, so I put on twenty pounds. On me it looks good.

Sure, you look fine. But you could wipe off some

of that lipstick. You're going to share it anyway—
with all those Morgans you got to kiss.

Caroline, blow your nose. And smile once in a
while, can't you?

Well, there it is—Aunt Sophie's estate. All twenty
acres of it. And don't be surprised if that'll be mine,
all mine, one day. Of course the house needs some
renovating. A new paint job. I'd put in another bath-
room—and a rumpus room in the basement. And on
the lawn I'd—

What are you screaming about, Millie? Huh?
Where? What sign? Well, now I saw everything!
Miss Sophie's Dog Hospital. Think it's a joke or some-
thing? But how could she?

Yeah, I'm thinking the same thing. Maybe everything the old girl has is—is going to the dogs. Of all
the sly tricks. Oh sure, she always had a hound or two
around, but I never gave it a thought. So that's why
she called this powwow. After driving two hundred
miles we're ruled out—just because our ears don't
flap.

There's the jolly clan now. Start waving, Millie.

Brother, do they look sad. I don't feel so good myself. I'd swap right now for the life of an Airedale.
Well, let's get out and mingle with the Morgans.

Smile, Caroline, and wave. Sure, Daddy is smiling
too. He's happy as a pup.

VENUS WITH A LABEL

Surrounded on all sides by beauty which can be bought in the jar, bottle, or whatever, is Miss Deborah Crockett, emissary of loveliness. Her temple of beauty is pitched among the miscellaneous wares of a department store. Looking ever so sleek and poised in her white satin smock, she is about to begin her demonstration.

Ladies, if you will gather in closer, we can begin the demonstration. This is absolutely free. You'll find it instructive, fascinating, and worth many times over the few minutes you'll spend listening to it. So will you please do me the courtesy of stepping in closer? Thank you.

That's right, madam. Bring the baby with you. One can't be too young or too old to learn new secrets for feminine charm.

You ladies over there in nighties. If you want to benefit from all this you must come closer. This is just a little confidential chat among us ladies. I can see you're all intelligent women, so if I may have a few moments of your time and step in a bit closer—Thank you very much.

Right here and now it might be well to introduce myself. I am Miss Crockett, and I represent the Glorianna Gibson line of cosmetics.

Now that we've become acquainted, let's begin our fascinating subject. It is fascinating because it's about ourselves. I mean *you, you* and *you.* Now if we can transform this *you* into a more attractive, desirable *you,* we certainly should do something about it, shouldn't we?

I'm sorry, madam. But the baby— Could you sort of quiet him—or her—or whatever? It is rather distracting. Thank you so much.

As I was saying, ladies, there is no need to be satisfied with just an ordinary face. All we have to do is to take our weapons of conquest in hand—our make-up—and improve upon nature. Just like—

Madam. Your baby is simply adorable—and the most adorable sounds come out of it. But after all, we both can't have all the attention. So— Yes, if you don't mind. Thank you so much. Bye, bye, baby. We're all going to miss you.

Well, now that we're one voice again—let's continue. I am holding in my hand a jar of my facial cleansing cream—Sensation. This is a basic treatment for every type of skin. And as I glance about I'd say that all the types are right before me. That is, the dry, the oily, the sensitive, and so forth. I gave a lecture in Boston last week, and out of an audience of five hundred or so, I'd say that about three ladies were normal—their complexions, I mean. That, of course, is no reflection upon dear old Boston, but on the individual herself.

Ah ah, little boy. Put that back. That's not for you. It's for ladies only, like your mother.

Will someone claim this child before— Oh, thank you, madam.

To continue. We take a generous dab of Sensation and apply some of it on our forehead—so—our cheeks—so—so—our chin—so—and by all means, the neck. How we've neglected it. And for our sin of omission, we can count all those dreadful rings, can't we? Almost as many as the brass ones some of those Ubangi women wear. The next—

Little boy, what are you doing? No, sweetheart, you can't eat it. Madam, will you— Yes, I see. He thought it whipped cream. Yes, too clever.

Now, all willing, we'll go on to the next step. The cream is applied, you see. And now to coax it into our pores and tissues. We start at the base—the throat— like this. Upward movement—caress yourself—up— up we go to our chin—and if we find two there, shame on you. Notice the rhythm as I massage. If you like, do it to music—something restful—like Debussy, would be lovely.

Hmm? No, madam. I wouldn't do it to jive. It might do something drastic.

Now our old friend, the nose. Be it Grecian, Roman, or whatever, we're going to get well acquainted with it. Now up to the noble brow. Up and over, up and over. And now—

Young lady, I don't need any sound effects with my demonstration. Do you mind snapping your chewing gum elsewhere? They're doing some riveting outside.

To continue, ladies, if you will.

Imagine now that twenty minutes have passed. We take our cleansing tissue in hand and remove the cream—like this—using the same movement in which it was applied. Start again at your throat and proceed upward. We are lifting away layers of grime which clogged our poor little pores.

When all the excessive cream is wiped away, to make the skin feel aglow and tingling, I use a quick dash of my astringent called Pick Me Up. And ladies, that's exactly what it does for you—within reason, of course.

Now we're ready to dress the face. Like a painter who selects his own colors, we must select our own individual shades to enhance our visual personality. Always think of your face as a shop window, where we put on display our most becoming wares, so that passers-by will stop, look and admire.

So what do I do about it? I consult my Glorianna Glamour Chart, which you all see here before you— and I groom my face according to my type. Now as you notice, I'm one of those in-betweens—not blonde and not brunette. So I look under the heading of Blonette and find my colors.

As you see, my pancake base is Blush of Spring. Notice how it blends into the skin tones so smoothly, giving a bewitching ivory finish. And so—

Goodness! Well, our little boy did it.

No, madam, it can't be scraped into another jar. Never mind about the pieces. Just do me a favor and handcuff the little monster.

But back to our demonstration. What is our most expressive feature? Anyone know? No, madam, not the tongue—although yours has been going constantly. Any other guesses? Our eyelashes? Not exactly, but we're getting warm. Our eyes. The windows of our soul, to be poetic. Now—

Madam, you're interrupting my— The window shade department? I haven't the slightest idea. But please go there, won't you?

Now for you ladies who are intelligent enough to listen, I'll continue. My eyeshadow, according to my type, is Blue Allure—which I use ever so sparingly in daytime—but with more abandon at night—like this. Then I use my eyebrow liner, Mystery—there— and now my eyes will do justice to any expression.

One last touch and our face is complete. Can you guess what it is? That's right, madam, the lips. And oh how tempting they can be, if we know just how. Again I consult my Glorianna Glamour Chart and find my shade. It's Murder Red. So I apply it like this—cheating a bit—making them fuller and riper, as my lips are rather thin—and there we are.

And so, ladies, as you see, the picture is complete. It is now ready to go on exhibition. All of you too can compete, if you remember that Glorianna Gibson is the "open sesame" to your door of beauty.

But remember this, ladies, we must stick to the colors mentioned on the chart all down the line. For instance, if you're blonde, you must use the shades suggested in your base, eyeshadow, and lipstick. You can't be Blush of Spring, Brazen Pink, and Hussy all in one. You understand?

To introduce Glorianna Gibson to you, and at a bargain offer too, the complete kit with the five items is only $5.98, including tax. So just raise your hands, ladies, and—

There's a lady over there. Does the lipstick stay on under water? Well, we never tried it on a deep sea diver, but it's an idea.

Anyone else? There's a hand. Yes, madam, you're Modesty. Oh, all you want is Pick Me Up? I'm sorry, but you must buy the complete kit.

Who is next? Yes, madam, your lipstick is Fire Alarm. Of course it's kiss-proof. You'll find out.

Anyone else? Just raise your hands, ladies, wave your money, and beauty is at your service.

POP SINGER

Jig Mason, one of the top platter singers, is being interviewed by a disc jockey in a radio studio. His voice has an exaggerated twang which could be described as "folksy." Since they will plug his new record, Jig delivers in his most affable style.

Thank you, Roy, for that fancy introduction. Afraid it's a little too buttery. Whenever anyone calls me a great pop singer, I always say to myself, "Jig, you're just a corn an' barley boy from Indiana. Don't let all this whoop-dee-doop go to that shaggy head of yours." But shucks, without my guitar by my side, I feel sorta tongue-tied. So why don't you feed me the quiz, Roy boy, an' I'll try to pitch back the answers.

That's right, Roy. I compose all the songs I sing. Oh, the tunes come real easy for me. Now take that song I did several months ago on the Spin Pin label. It's called, in case a few of you didn't hear of it, *Throw Me a Wiggle.* All I did was borrow a few bars from *The Old Oaken Bucket* an' reverse 'em—add a couple chords from *Yankee Doodle,* an' the last six bars of *Listen to the Mocking Bird* in a rhythm beat —an' out came *Throw Me a Wiggle.* Yes, Roy, since you said it first, it was on the Pop Platter Parade for twelve weeks. An' if I may add, almost a million *Wiggles* have been sold. It helped the chiropractors along.

I'm real glad you asked that, Roy. Yes, I got a spankin' new record out—an' I just happen to have a platter with me. It's for you, Roy, with my compliments. An' I won't mind a bit if you read the title out loud. That's right. It's called *You Break Me Into Bits, Baby*. It's a long title—but I thought it a switch from the one on the flip side. That's called *Plop*.

Well, since you ask me—yes, Roy, I am working on a new one. It's a bouncy number. Right now it's called *The Ash Can Jump*—but I may change it to somethin' like *Wham—That's My Heart*.

That question is asked a lot—did I ever take singin' lessons? Shucks, I thought it showed—that I didn't, I mean. All I did was save my grocery stamps, swap them in for a guitar, an' just do what come naturally.

Now I know you're anxious to play my new record for the folks. An' for those who just tuned it—do you want to tell them that I'm Jig Mason on this end—an' that my new record is just out—an' that it's called *You Break Me Into Bits, Baby?* Thanks, pal. My middle name is Plug.

While you're spinnin' my record, I better whiz on down to your record shop—the one slab dab on the square. That's it, Roy. The Melody Box. I'll be there for the next two hours. So come on down, folks. I'll have my pen with me, so I'll be glad to autograph my records. An' if a pretty girl asks me, I can write my name on my picture. I'll have a few with me. A few hundred, I mean.

That reminds me of a funny thing that happened the other day. I forget the name of the town. On this crazy tour I show up in two or three a day. Anyhow, this cute girlie steps up, asks for my autograph, an' sticks out her two thumbs. So that's where I wrote it. Jig on the one nail an' Mason on the other. She said she wouldn't wash her thumbs for weeks.

Well, Roy, I can't let all those fans of mine wait around any longer. It was real neighborly of you to let me stop by an' chat with your listeners. An' they sure can make me happy by puttin' the needle on me an' spinnin' me round an' round. But if they don't— *You Break Me Into Bits, Baby*. Well, flap my ears. That just happens to be the name of my new record. This is Jig Mason on this end, sayin' "Keep happy an' stay with it."

MISS PRUNELLA THATCHER

A herd of humans, willing volunteers for a smatter-ing of culture, have banded together in an imposing wing of a museum. Miss Prunella Thatcher, authority on modern art and looking it, approaches the group. Her poised, all-knowing manner teeters just a trifle as she addresses them.

Good afternoon, dear art lovers. Are all of you wait-ing to hear the gallery talk? Splendid. What a large and inspiring group you are. I'm Miss Prunella Thatcher. It'll be my pleasure to escort you on our little art tour.

But before we start, just a word about the pictures you're about to see. They're all modern. To define—they're studies in cubism, expressionism, abstraction, non-objective, and so forth. But don't let these terms frighten you, if you've never heard them before. And apropos of that, how many of you have never seen a modern painting? Raise your hands, please. Ah, most of you haven't, I see. How I envy you—to experience for the first time the joy of it all.

Are we ready to begin our picturesque journey? Fine. We'll do only the south wing—just enough to whet your artistic appetite. But if your soul is starved for more, you'll find another collection in the north wing. Come, come, we're on our way. Follow me, please.

Here we are. Now, this picture is a little startling to begin with perhaps, but we may as well immerse ourselves completely at the very start. It is called *Night Ecstatic*. It is non-objective. That is, dear people, it has no definite form. It is purely emotional. Look at it, absorb it, and see what it does for you.

Some of you, I see, are amused by it. Indicating that it has a definite emotional effect. Notice how those vivid reds whirl about—there—there—and there. Do you feel the rhythm of it? And those lush greens. See how they balance the circles of lemon yellow. A bacchanal of color, isn't it?

Now if any questions come to your mind, I'll be glad—

Yes, madam? Well that is a clever deduction, but I don't believe the artist had a traffic light in mind. This is merely an emotional release expressed through an artistic medium, you see?

What, little man? Why, yes, they do look like lollipops, don't they?

All right, good people, if you can tear yourselves away, we'll go on to our next painting.

This is a refreshing example of expressionism called *Ducklings on Pond*. Notice the rustic effect the artist has captured. The suggestion of trees over there—the meadow there—and the pond down along here. Now I know you're puzzled as to where the dear little ducklings can be. Shall I tell you? They swam down the stream a bit, out of sight. Isn't that droll?

Have you a question, madam? No, those aren't green noodles. That represents the verdant meadow. You see, that's the beauty of expressionisms. They can suggest any number of things.

Yes, madam. That blue mass up there is the sky with clouds. It looks like what? Really? Well, next time you wear your blue scarf with the holes in it, think of this painting, won't you?

On to our next picture. Here is a beguiling little study in cubism called *Futility in Flight*. A study of geometrical designs artistically arranged to give us esthetic pleasure. It took the artist, Anton Druski, three years to complete it. Poor man, after devoting an entire lifetime creating beauty such as this, died a pitiful pauper. Can you imagine that? Oh, you can. Well, my good man, that is your opinion. There's opposition here between the squares and triangles, you see.

Wish to say something, madam? How amusing. Did you all hear that? It reminds this lady of Junior's toys all over the floor.

Come along, please. Are we all together? Oh, there seem to be less of us. Well, the chaff from the wheat, they always say.

Now here is a rather bizarre item labelled *Asphyxia.* Intriguing title, isn't it? It probably demonstrates the emotion one feels while being asphyxiated. I really wouldn't know.

What, madam? Oh, no indeed. The artist is still very much alive. He is Pierre Chicano, lives in Great Neck, I believe, and is the father to seven little Chicanos.

Rather morbid, isn't it? The painting, I mean. But that is the effect the artist intended. This too is non-objective. Splashes of color on canvas to arouse a response in us. Does it, dear people?

What, little man? Isn't that clever. I never thought of that—like measles in different colors.

How's that, madam? Really? Well, if your six-year-old daughter can do better than that, she's a positive genius.

I fully realize, good people, that perhaps some of these modernisms are too extreme for some of us. They may appear trivial to some, childlike to others, and to some, I'm afraid, ludicrous. But let's not be too censorious. Instead let us have one little ounce of tolerance. Modern art will win you over, if you give it a chance. Don't shake your head, madam. It will, if you meet it half way, so to speak.

But we mustn't tarry. On we go.

This impressionistic jumble is called *Bedelia.* Tantalizing, isn't it. And why, you wonder, call it *Bedelia?* Ah, *cherchez la femme,* you know. Here the

artist represents no superficial portrait of fleshy fea-
tures—but has probed beneath and exposed an inner
Bedelia—by the use of various symbols. For instance,
that grey, curly blob suggests the head of a lamb—
meaning a gentle disposition. That bundle of dollar
bills on the wing means that Bedelia is a spendthrift.
Do you see that wriggly mass over there? What does
it suggest to you? Spaghetti? Very clever. But I see
it as a snake—her other nature—her dual personality
—the vixen in her. Let's pick out a few other traits.
There is a deck of cards twisted around an alarm
clock. That means Bedelia is pleasure loving. That
hyacinth growing out of an old shoe suggests un-
requited love, and so forth. So for a bit of self-analy-
sis, ladies, ask yourselves the question, "How much
of Bedelia is in me?"

On to our next study. Just a few more, dear people,
and then we've completed the wing.

Here is— Oh my. Just three of you left. What
strength of characters you have, dear ladies.

Here we have another example of eubism called
Infinity. Be careful, ladies, before it weaves a spell
on you. Those scintillating colors twisting in and out
have almost an hypnotic effect. Poor Gregane, the
artist, had a wretched time balancing all of this. So
much so that it completely unbalanced him—if you
know what I mean. But before it whisks you away,
ladies, let us—

Why, I do believe it has. Where are the other two? I see. Well, let's continue, shall we?

I do believe this is the last picture. *Foolish Patience* is what the artist calls it. A fetching little abstraction, isn't it?

Really? I'm so glad you like it. It's one of my favorites, too. And now, madam, may I ask your name? Congratulations, Mrs. Plunkett. May I shake your hand? Why? For being so firm of purpose, that's why. In the six months that I've been conducting these gallery talks, you, my dear, are the first person who has stayed with me to the last. A true art lover to the very end, that's what you are, Mrs. Plunkett.

You don't say! You painted this—*Foolish Patience?* Of course! Then you must be Cynthia Plunkett. How thrilling! I must tell Miss Hemingway right away. And the Board of Directors will be simply elated. They'll all want to meet you. We may even be rash and have cocktails. Right this way, my dear Mrs. Plunkett.

FATHER HAS A PROBLEM

For the past ten minutes Mr. Bradford has been having a hectic time trying to engage a baby-sitter for the evening. With a hopeless shrug, he plunks down the telephone.

Well, Ethel, that's the third refusal. Peg. She sprained her wrist in gym today. She twirled her baton the wrong way. So tonight she must soak her hand. I tried to, dear—even said we had a basin, plenty of hot water, and epsom salts. But she'd rather do it at home.

Sorry, Michael. Daddy hasn't time to play now. I must dial a girl friend for you. Ethel, watch him a minute, will you? There, Michael. Go over to Mommy.

Of all times for Judy to let us down—to call it off the last minute like this. Funny that her sister decided to have a birthday party all of a sudden.

Let's see—I have three more names to go. I'm dialing Nancy Phelps in the next block. Yes, I know, dear. Nancy giggles a lot. But who can be finicky when—

Hello. Is Nancy there? . . . No, Mrs. Phelps, I'm not calling for a date. This is Mr. Bradford. I won-

dered if Nancy would baby sit tonight. . . . Oh, I
see . . . Yes, I heard she was giving one. Well,
thanks all the same. Goodbye.

No luck. Nancy and her giggles are going to that
birthday party. Good grief! Look at the time! We
have to leave in half an hour. Hurry and get dressed,
will you?

And why didn't you check with Judy this morning?
You know how much this dinner date means to me.
Gillmore is top man in his field. I've been trying to
pin down a date for months. I had it all on the line.
After cocktails and a steak dinner Gillmore would
beam. Then I'd casually mention how I would pro-
mote that mayonnaise account. And before you could
say Gillmore, Gibson and Schultz, Incorporated, up
pops a bonus. But—

Watch it, Ethel! Michael picked up your mirror.

Suppose I give Sally Lewis a buzz. Here goes.
What, Ethel? Why don't you like Sally? Okay, I'll
tell her not to use the phone. All right, all right, I'll
tell her that too—no boy friends around.

Hello. Is Sally there? Thank you.

Wow. You never looked like that before. A new
dress, huh? Oh sure, it's dazzling. And so is the price,
I'm sure. Of course, Ethel, you want to look as attractive as Mrs. Gillmore. But did you—

Hello. Sally? This is Mr. Bradford. How about a
date with Michael tonight? Soon—within twenty
minutes or so. Oh, I see. Well, can't you wrap a towel

around your head and— Huh? A permanent wave—
at your age? Well, could you do it tomorrow night? I
see. Who? Linda Watson? No, she's never been here.
What's her number? Okay, I have it. Thanks, Sally.

That checks off Sally. Say, how early do kids begin
this glamour business? She is getting a bronze rinse
and a wave.

Well, who's next on the list? Doris. Let's see if
she— Huh? Now why don't you like Doris? Oh,
Ethel, how do you know she snoops around? Okay,
so she spilled your perfume on the rug. It probably
was good for the moths. Very well, dear, I won't call
her. Suggest someone else then, if you—

Wow! There. Michael did it. I told you, Ethel, to
take away that mirror. Haven't we enough on our
minds without having a smashed mirror around?

Well, that takes care of the list—unless I call
Linda. She's the girl Sally spoke about. May as well
try her number and— I know, Ethel. I feel the same
way about having a strange girl here. But— Oh, her
line is busy.

If we can't reach Linda we'll just have to take
Michael over to the Olsens'. I know, dear. They're not
fond of children. I'll take along a bottle of Scotch to
ease the pain. I'll try that number again. There. It's
ringing.

Hello. Linda? No, this isn't Droopy. It's Mr. Bradford. Sally suggested that I call you. We need a baby
sitter right away, and if you— What? The baby's

name is Michael. He's no trouble at all. How old? Michael is almost two. Just see that he goes to bed by— Oh, of course you may turn on television. Look, Linda, can you be ready by— What? Yes, we have cokes in the refrigerator. I'll pick you up by— Why yes, you may help yourself to a snack. So if you can be— How's that? No, we don't have a dog. Sorry. Oh. Well, I'd rather you wouldn't bring it along. Oh, he does. Just a moment, please.

Ethel, listen to this. Linda wants to bring along her boxer. A dog yet. She says Champ is real cuddly. Afraid I can't talk her out of it. Champ goes everywhere Linda goes—like Mary and her lamb. Well, you could take all the bric-a-brac from the tables. Oh sure, Champ will probably smash a lamp or two. I suppose it's what you call an occupational hazard. So let's risk it, huh?

Okay, Linda. I'll pick the two of you up. Can you be ready in fifteen minutes? Well, could you speed up supper? Mrs. Bradford and I must be at the Hotel Royal by seven. All right then—in twenty minutes. What's your address? Right. I'll honk the horn.

Now I ask you—what will baby sitters demand next? All they want to do is look at television—gab on the phone—raid the ice box—and in their spare time look after Junior.

Yes, Ethel, I'm ready. Just comb my hair again and—

The phone. Who's calling about what? Will you

answer it, Ethel? Afraid it's Linda with a baby ele-
phant.

Who is it? Yes, I'm free tomorrow evening. Why?

Okay, now who was that? Mrs. Gillmore. Now
don't tell me they can't— Oh no! Well, that's great.
So the push-button executive has an out-of-town
conference, has he? A fine time to call it off.

Well, Ethel, you may as well shed the glitter and
start dinner. Yes, dear, I'll round up a sitter for tomorrow. Certainly not. Linda and her pooch can stay
put. Here's the list. Think I'll take it in alphabetical
order and see what happens. B for Betty. Here we go
again.

STRANGE SISTER

In a rugged cabin, such as can be found amid the hills of Kentucky, a woman of tattered and careworn appearance, is doing her daily chores. Wearily she shambles to the door, then turns, and in a tired drone speaks to a bare-legged girl.

Abbie, watch them taters so they don't burn to nothin'. I'm agoin' out fer some beets—ef they hain't all dried up. The ground is somethin' turrible. Reckon it won't rain agin today.

Now what's Pepper barkin' fer?

Well, I declare! Ef thar hain't someone comin' up the pasture. A woman—it looks like to me. Can't make out who it be. Ef them specs of mine was fixed, I could— Kin you, Abbie? No, never seed the likes of her before. Looks like one of 'em pack peddlers— her a-carryin' that bag. Look at that dress, Abbie. Like what them ladies wear in that Sears-Roebuck book of ourn. 'Cept she hain't so young or purty. Go in, Abbie, an' bring out that chair—the one Clint Baskin set on last time he come by. I'll set out here on the stoop.

Hush up, Pepper!

Put it over thar, Abbie—in the shade. Now ya better go in an' keep an eye on them taters.

Mornin' thar! Yes, 'tis kinda warm fer May. Won't ya have a chair an' rest awhile. Ya look tuckered out.

Down, Pepper, down.

She don' like strangers none. But— Well, I declare. Look at her a-lickin' yer hand. She carries on like she knew ya.

Git down, Pepper.

Shore, set right over thar. 'Tain't often we git company up here. Seems like no one come by but peddlers—'bout every spring. But you be the first lady peddler come traipsin' round. How ya git here? The lane hain't wide enough ter drive up. Oh, the bus brought ya. I seed them things scat down the road like a chariot of thunder. But that's a good mile yonder. No wonder ya is warm an' tuckered out. Reckon a dipper of water would taste pow'ful good.

Abbie! Bring out a dipperful.

My, them flies is pesky today. Mebbe it means rain. That corn patch is just a-beggin' fer it.

Give it to the lady, Abbie.

Poor young un—she's mighty shy before strangers —like she hain't got no tongue in her head.

All right, Abbie, go in an' stir them taters.

Mercy, naw. She hain't my daughter. Jest drink yer fill. Her folk lived down the lane apiece. They's dead now. So I took Abbie. An' she can be handy— when she's a mind ter. 'Spect I'd be pow'ful lonesome without her.

Naw, I hain't never had no husband. Jest hain't had
no time fer actin' up like young uns do. Thar was
always a heap ter do. Ever since I kin 'member Maw
was sick. Her one side stiff as a fence rail—fer nigh
unto twenty year. So thar was cookin' ter do, milk
ole Bess, a-sewin' after supper, an'--

But lan' sakes. My tongue is a-goin' like butter. Bin
a spell since a body come jest to set. Now 'spose ya
tell me 'bout yerself. Whar ya come from anyhow?
Chicagi? Ya don' say. My sister live thar. Her name's
Lilac. We call her that 'cause the day she was born
them lilacs started a-bloomin'. She was younger than
me—an' purty. Hair so yeller—somethin' like yours.
Don' s'pose ya met her—in Chicagi? Lilac Barton.
I reckon it must be so big ya cain't meet everyone
thar.

Now some folks is jest meant to be plain, know
pow'ful little of nothin', an' jest work—like me. But
Lilac—she was diff'rent. Since jest a mite she was
meant to be a lady. Why, she traipsed ter school
every day—five mile it were—over to Beaver Hill.
But that larnin' jest made her hungry fer more. She
had a hankerin' ter get everythin' she could—an'
mighty quick. So with the money I git fer crops, an'
sewin' I did fer folks, she goes to Louisville—ter a
high school thar. Then she took it in her head ter go
ter Chicagi—an' git some fancy job.

Aw, naw, I never reckon it like that. Didn' mind

workin' hard fer her. 'Tain't everybody kin have a
sister like her—so smart, an' purty. An' she is happy
—thar in Chicagi. Git a letter now an' then—with
ten dollar. Will Larkin, who gits the mail in the village, read 'em ter me. My eyes ain't so spry any
more.

Lilac never say what she's a-doin'. But I know it
be somethin' mighty good—'cause she told about
jew'lry, an' fancy dresses, an' purty things like that.
My, you look awful fancy too. Reckon all ladies dress
up like they was goin' ter a party—even ef they
hain't—in Chicagi.

But Lilac never come back. She left a mighty long
time ago. Pepper here was jest a pup when she went
away. An' now poor Pepper is almost blind. Just cain't
figger out why she don' ever come back to see me.
She promise me that one day—

What ya say? Aw, no. Lilac would never do that.
She'd never make up to folks what wasn't proper.
'Tain't much I could larn her, but I brung her up
good. She done read her Bible every evenin' an'—

I don' know why yer talkin' agin her like this—
when ya never knowed her. Even ef she hankered
after them fancy things—as city folk do—she'd never
do nothin' bad ter git 'em. Even ef she couldn't help
a-goin' bad—like ya say—she jest wouldn't. Not Lilac.

She's a-comin' back one day—a fine lady. Every
mornin' I look down the pasture an' wonder ef today

she'll come back. I'll know her—even afore she says a word.

How I'll know? 'Cause she'll be like I always see her, that's how. The good don' git old an' ugly. She hain't forgit me. She'll come back, I know. Guess I'm jest a-livin' on till she do.

My, I don' know why I'm a-tellin' ya this—stranger like ya be. Guess it's been inside fer so long it jest had to bust out. But yer bein' from Chicagi—well— ya jest made me think of Lilac.

Ye hain't cryin', are ya? Oh, I see. Ya got a cold. That sweat on yer face looks almost like yer cryin'. Mebbe ya'd like to wash up a bit. I'll call Abbie.

Abbie! Abbie!

Now what could that young un be doin'? May as well do it myself, I reckon.

Abbie! Oh, there ya are. Bring out the basin with water, an' some soap, an' that thar meal sack. It's a-hangin' on the line. How are them taters fryin'? They smell real good. An' pour a mite more milk on that corn. Ef our fixin's are good enough mebbe we'll have company—ef we ask the lady nice-like.

Ya heard what I jest said to Abbie. Would ya like to stay fer—

Well, I be! Did ya ever! Look, Abbie. She's a-goin' down the pasture fast as all git-out. She hain't even say goodbye nor nothin'. Ef some folks hain't ornery.

What ya got thar, Abbie? Yep, guess she dropped it. Lemme see. My, it's a purty han'kerchief. What does it say thar in the corner? It's sewed real fancy-like. "L"? That's fer her name, I reckon—whatever it might be.

Well, we cain't fret 'bout it—with all them things ter do. Git a bunch of beets, Abbie, while I fix up them taters.

ACTOR SUMMER-STYLE

*The scene is backstage in the Holly Ridge Theatre.
Mark Weston, the star of the week, is impeccably
dressed for the performance, and carries on a mirror
which he props up and glances in at frequent inter-
vals to adjust tie, comb hair again, and check make-
up. He renders unrehearsed dialogue with various
members of the troupe.*

How's the house tonight, Frank? A little over half?
Well, all it takes is five minutes to fill it up—as my
shows always do. Last summer I did capacity everywhere—except for the week of Esther. She was that
hurricane we had.

(*Slaps his hand*) Damn these mosquitoes! They're
for critics. Why didn't they go on tour with last
week's star. Yes, I mean Lola Pearson. Only too well,
my boy. I still pay her alimony—when she isn't working—which is most of the time.

Got a cigarette? I really broke the habit—but
comes curtain time there's that old craving. Thanks,
Frank. No filter tip? Sorry. Ask that little Mitzi child,
will you? She smokes them—takes happy pills, too—
and is all of sixteen.

Five minutes? Thank you, Gary. Hmm? Yes, I'll do

another picture in September. And after ten weeks of *How Bitter The Grape* it'll be a rest cure.

Frankly, I despise this show. My agent did a colossal job of over-playing. And then every week I'm at the mercy of a different leading lady. I use the term loosely. Next year I'll do a package deal. By the end of summer everybody hates everybody, but you're spared second-rate surprises like this Webb wench. Wherever did Leon find her? Really? Well, if she ever played opposite Evans, it was just long enough to hand him a cup of tea. Playing a maid is the extent of her histrionic ability. What is her first name? I always want to call her Jezebel. Of course. It's Julia.

Oh, here's Mitzi. Can you spare it, honey? Light, please. Thank you, darling. I'll buy you a carton before I leave.

By the way, Gary, do you think Leon is catching the show tonight? Well, I'll risk it. And since you're holding the book, I'll let you in on it. I'm changing the blocking with Julia in the second act. Okay, so I have an expressive back, as Leon says. I refuse to stand like a stick of furniture while Julia has those long speeches. You know, how she relates those weird dreams she had. There the direction is all wrong. So I'll do it like I did last week at the Cape. I'll cross to the window, wave to someone outside, go to the bar and mix a drink. It perks up the scene no end. And then—

Oh, hello, Betty. You're just on cue. Look dear, I'm doing a little change in our scene. Remember those two speeches of mine that Leon cut? Well, they're in tonight. Why those two speeches are the key to the whole scene. They give me the motivation to make that phone call. Now don't panic, darling. Let Leon blow his top. I'll join him.

Pardon me, dear. I want to speak to props. What's her name? Oh yes, Liza.

Liza? Oh, there you are. Aha, I caught you. Mustn't eat the props, you know. Liza, did you put the revolver in the top desk drawer? You're positive? It better be. I felt awfully stupid committing murder with that ball point pen. And then Tom dashes on and says, "I heard the shot." Well, as you know, it was a farce from then on.

Oh, good evening, Miss Tuttle. I'm sorry. Certainly I'll call you Gwendolyn. What, dear? Oh; you're doing the part superbly. No, I couldn't suggest a thing. Just be your sweet, enchanting self. Excuse me. I must speak to the stage manager about something.

Gary, do me a favor and keep that Tuttle woman out of my greying hair. Last night after every exit, there was Gwendolyn with a tender greeting. Will you remind her that I go for ingenues only. It seems in every town I play there's a plump dowager who has to be convinced. Yes indeed. Gwendolyn makes the most of her lines—all five of them. And her exit is really extravagant. The way she prolongs it in the doorway. I thought she was waiting for applause. But we must humor her. I hear she's throwing a party tonight and that her bar is really loaded.

Places? I'm ready.

That's another flaw in this play. I'm on too soon. There's no build-up of expectancy—which a star deserves. Now if I ever wrote a play, I'd have a different approach. At the opening, for at least ten minutes, the dialogue would be about me. Then I'd make a spectacular entrance. And then for some reason which I haven't figured out yet, all the actors would pantomime for the remainder of the play. From then on there'd be just one speaking part. Mine, of course. There. Did O'Neill ever think of that?

Well, where is Miss Mediocrity? I can hardly wait for her to stink up the stage. Last night Julie had a de luxe Italian dinner—and the garlic lingered on. Then she wondered why I broke the clinch so quickly. Well, that won't happen again. I made a deal with props. Tonight her glass of Scotch will be straight Listerine. But not a word to—

Ah, here comes the flower of my delight now. Good evening, Julia. Late again, darling. We're holding curtain for you.

Okay, Gary. Let's go.

After you, my sweet. And remember, on my entrance, hold for the applause. They love me out there.

THE LADY IS TAURUS

The day for Mr. and Mrs. Webb is barely a half-hour old, as Susan Webb enters her sunlit dining room. She greets Margaret, her housemaid, and her husband, Fred, who is shielded by the morning newspaper. Mrs. Webb carries a sheaf of mimeographed papers with an air of importance.

Good morning, Margaret. Just grapefruit juice, toast, and coffee for me. No butter. Counting calories again this week.

Fred, have you had your eggs and toast? Fred, I asked if— Never mind. I see you haven't. And must you growl like that? But little wonder—digesting all those grim headlines before breakfast the way you do. All right, so I'm not a realist. At least I can start my day with a smile instead of—

Oh, what lovely shoes. Lift the paper a little higher, will you? At Butterfields. And they're reduced too. Oh, there. You would turn the page.

It seems to me, Fred, you could start off the day to better advantage. And Doctor Zombo thinks so too. Who is he? If you'd glance at the society page once in a while you'd know that he spoke for our

Cosmic Club last evening. My, he was magnetic.
And such a fascinating subject. Well, you might ask
what it was. Really, Fred, I may as well be talking to
the sugar bowl for all the—

Thank you. His subject was *You and the Zodiac*.
Don't be stupid, Fred. Astrology. He's nothing of the
kind. Anything the least bit cultural or psychic you
call phony. Yes, you do. Besides, he looks more dashing in a bow tie than you do. Where in heaven's name
did you pick that one?

All right, Fred, all right. It's on *your* neck. Ever
since you went to that college reunion your ties and
socks have been blazing. But I understand, dear.
It's just a phase you're going through. Men have
them too.

That's fine, Margaret. Just the toast for me. You
might ask Mr. Webb if he wants more coffee. Never
mind asking—just fill his cup. That'll be all, Margaret.

And now to read your horoscope. Did you know
you're Scorpio? You are, dear. Scorpio. It's your sign
in the zodiac. Because you were born on November
9th, that's why. Certainly I bought it. One for you
and one for me. By the way, Doctor Zombo said we
were perfectly mated. No, silly, you and me. Because
of our elements. Yours is water and mine is earth.
Now listen to what it says about you.

It says: "If you are a Scorpion you like to rule the
roost and expect obedience from others." I certainly
agree. "You're not sentimental but have real sym-

pathy." That's nice to know. "You can succeed in such occupations as physician, nurse, druggist, musician—" Too bad you gave away your trombone. —"writer, officer in army or navy." Goodness, aren't you versatile? And to think you're merely an accountant.

Pass the cream, please. Have you noticed—I've cut down from two dashes to one.

Now let's see what your stars predict for today. As Doctor Zombo said, "Fit the right day to the right deed." May 6th. Here we are. "Proceed with caution in monetary affairs this morning." Oh dear. And I wanted you to be a darling and let me buy draperies for the living room. Well, I'll have to ask you again —on the right day. And then it says: "You profit tonight." I suppose that means you're playing poker with the boys.

I ask you, can anything be more dreary than dry toast? Pass the jam, please. A few calories more or less won't matter.

Now let's read about my day. Of course, I'm under a different sign. Well, I didn't suspect it myself, but I'm Taurus, the Bull.

Now really, Fred. I don't think it's that funny. Look —coffee all over your sleeve. Now how can it be *my* fault when *you* did the laughing. I merely said— Well, if this is all so jolly we should consult our horoscopes every morning—like Doctor Zombo advised.

Listen to this. "You have a fine mind"—meaning

me—"practical common sense, and a strong will." Doesn't he say the nicest things? "You are not fond of work." Well, that I dispute. "You can win success as an engineer, a fireman, a teacher, or a secretary." And to think I worked in a dress shop all those years. Then it says, "Avoid rich food. You are apt to be overweight this month." Oh dear. And I was just about to have some of that Danish pastry. It looks delicious.

Now let's see what is my destiny for today. Here we are. "You are close to the bottom of your lunar cycle—" That sounds dreadful. "—so don't accept any business or social obligations. Stay indoors in solitude—write those letters—clean those closets—or stick to your knitting. By all means avoid Gemini people today."

Well, that's that. Of course I'm going to follow it through. I've had all sorts of things planned for today but I'll cancel them. If the stars forbid who am I to challenge them? All right, Fred, so it's phooey. You can scoff all you wish. I might have known you'd be mulish.

I can look at it all objectively. Instead of having lunch with Pamela, and see a silly movie, I can stay home and accomplish little things that count. I can finish the sweater for Janet's baby. Write a letter to Aunt Alice, and— I wonder if she's Gemini? Her birthday is March 18th. Heavens, we didn't even send her a card.

Let's see. The signs are all listed here. No. Aunt Alice is Pisces, the Fishes.

That bun makes me drool. And stop smacking your lips like that, Fred. It's cruel.

Oh, thank you, Margaret. Want more coffee, Fred?

By the way, Margaret, are you Gemini? Of course you don't. I mean, when were you born—what month? February 9th. Let's see. You're Aquarius, the Water Bearer. How appropriate. Only it happens to be coffee at the moment. Will you bring in the phone, Margaret? I want to make a few calls.

Dinner the same time, Fred? All right. I haven't the slightest notion what it'll be. Oh, Fred, don't you want to leave your wallet with me? See. You've forgotten already. Your horoscope said that— Never mind. Goodbye, dear.

No, nothing more for me, Margaret. Plug in the phone, will you, please? You can clear away now. Yes, it's a gorgeous morning. No, Margaret, I'm going to stay indoors and be domestic. Don't bother about lunch for me. All I dare have is a tossed salad.

I must call Pamela first of all. I wonder if she's Gemini? Nothing, Margaret. Just my usual morning gibberish.

Pamela? Susan . . . Just fine. Pamela, before we're engulfed in a topic, let me ask if— What, dear? Of course, Pamela, I remember our date. And I was calling to say that I must beg off because— . . . Yes, it would be a divine day for a drive in the country. But I have things to do here at— No, I've never been to the Bide-a-Wee Inn. I understand their lobster is exquisite. But I'm afraid it's much too rich for— Really? How nice that Florence and Polly can go along. I wonder if they're Gemini? . . . Nothing, Pamela.

Yes, canasta on the terrace would be fun. I'd love to go, Pamela, but my horoscope says— . . . Pamela, you aren't listening to a word I'm saying . . . Oh, never mind. All right, I can be ready by one . . . Fine. Goodbye, Pamela.

Oh, Margaret. My plans are altered. I'm going out for the day. It's much too glorious to be cloistered indoors. I'm going upstairs and dress. And about dinner, I'll have an enormous lunch, so a salad will do for me. Broil two chops for Mr. Webb with tomatoes or something.

And by the way, Margaret, if you haven't a thing to do, you might straighten up those closets. And for amusement, if you'd like to knit, there's that baby sweater in the lower desk drawer. But remember to knit a little tighter, won't you, so our stitches will match?

What, Margaret? Oh yes, our horoscopes. Just put them in the living room with the magazines. I'll look at them again some other time.

SHORT ACQUAINTANCES

(As seen around Times Square)

SIGHT-SEEING GUIDE

See Wall Street—Chinatown—uptown—downtown
—all around town. Sight-seein'.

How about it, lady! Bus leaves in five minutes. Ya
wanna tell your friends back home all about it. In
two short hours ya'll go more places than—

Huh? From Brooklyn. Whada ya know. Okay, I'm
sold. Ya speak the lango. I'm from Flatbush myself.

See all the sights around the city. Bus leaves in five
minutes.

How about takin' the wife, Mister? Huh? Oh, all
right. So she's another guy's wife. Ya both can see
the— Huh? The Automat? Across the street. Now I
tell ya what ya do. Go have a snack—get rid of those
nickels—an' then come back for a tour. I'll look for ya.

Hurry, folks. Bus leaves in five minutes. All around
Noo Yawk.

What, lady? The bus station? Half a block that way.
Bus to where? Wilmerding? Never heard of it. It
sounds like the end of the line.

See all the sights around the city. Bus leaves in five minutes. See Radio City—United Nations—Riverside Drive—

Okay, Harry, take over. No customers. I'm gonna see a tall glass of beer.

MISS STAGE-STRUCK

Here it is, Joan—Broadway at night—and much better than in technicolor. Let's pretend it's all ablaze just for us. I can't believe it either—to think we're actually here. Me too. I'm tingling. Let's stand here for a few minutes and stare.

So do I—feel exactly like the pop-eyed country cousin. But I don't mind. It's wonderful. And to think that all these streets have theatres—and that I'll be acting in one of them before long.

Just imagine, Joan, how well we'll know New York say—a year from now. And wouldn't it be fun to know what we'll be doing? You'll be modeling—for only the best magazines, of course. I'll be out of dramatic school by then and giving my name to every producer in the book.

Of course I'll probably be just a walk-on in the first

show or two. But when I'm twenty-one or so, I'll be a Broadway star or know the reason why.

What, Joan? All right. Let's walk up Broadway. Aren't you head over heels in love with it? And it's all ours, Joan—that's the wonderful part. Think of all the celebrities living here. They'll just have to move over and make room for two more.

Let's go across the street and gawk some more.

TRUCK DRIVER ON FOOT

Aw, quit givin' me that. Look Sadie, I told ya—I didn't even see that blonde tomato. All right. So she was havin' a drink at the bar—an' we was over at the table. Okay, okay. It's my fault she gave me the look. That's the way ya want it.

Come on, Sadie, zip it up. Look, what movie shall it be? Huh? Aw, that one sounds gooey. Let's see one of them murder ones. Anyways, ya seem in the mood —givin' me the big blast.

Aw, go ahead an' burn. Jeeze, back in the same groove. Listen, Sadie, I tol' ya why we couldn't date last night. All the way from Columbus Circle what did I tell ya? That's right. The truck broke down.

Bein' stuck in Bear Mountain was no daisy pickin' for me. An' don't ask, "Who's Daisy?"

An' like I says, I gave ya a ring from that gas station but your line went buzz buzz. For all I know maybe you was fixin' up somethin' with another guy. Jeeze, if I was a jealous Elmer I could put the quiz on you, too.

Look, here's a pitcher show. Let's go in. Huh? Okay, so it's romantic. I'll look at anythin' if it'll keep ya from flippin' the lip.

LADY, EAST SIDE

Sheila, be a darling and charm along a cab. You do it so beautifully. My, don't you loathe all this Broadway rabble? But what *can* one do? One has to be seen at opening nights. Really, if it wasn't for the theatre and the operas, I'd never wag a finger west of Fifth Avenue.

Here come a flock of cabs. Just keep waving, Sheila, and see what happens.

Don't remind me. We just saw *the* colossal fizzle of the season. That play was neither smart, risqué, or dirty. Just atrocious.

Which reminds me—did Stephanie Whitecap invite you to her musicale tomorrow? No? Oh, Sheila, you have all the luck. After the last one I swore in blood never again. But then Stephanie rings you, showers all sorts of flattering things in your ear—and before you know it, you're trapped—*but* trapped. I'm afraid Stephanie plays piano with more bravado than she is a virtuoso. One could forgive all with a few Martinis about. But to make it utterly dismal, it's always tea.

Wave at that one, Sheila. Perhaps— Oh, dear. It's taken.

What, Sheila? So do I. I feel absolutely irascible. I can hardly wait to slip into my negligee, take a tranquilizer, and dip into that book I told you about. It's utterly devastating. The author is half Egyptian and half Norwegian. And—

Guess who's over there. Lola Watson. And looking as gaudy as ever. Certainly not. She's off my list. After that poisonous rumor she circulated about—

Lola darling! You look simply divine. Yes, it's been an eternity since I saw you. Do ring me and we'll have lunch.

What a hasty departure. No wonder, with that dashing escort. She might have introduced him. I wonder why she avoided— You think so? Of course. If I know Lola, he's the husband of someone we know. A brazen vulturess, that's what she is.

Oh, there's a cab. Wave, Sheila. You did it. Come along, darling.

FIVE AN' DIME DOLL

Yeah, Agnes, ain't it sensational? But wait till ya hear the rest. So after I keeps him guessin' about givin' him a date, see? Yeah, the cute marine. Well, he's hangin' around, polishin' off a line about bein' lost an' lonely, an' what I'd have on after five—when who should wiggle out of the drain but Mr. Quinley. Yeah, he's the assistant manager—an' a bunion. So he anchors over too, see, an' takes it all in.

So I says to the marine, under my breath like. I says, "Look, ya better buy somethin' or shove off. We're bein' X-rayed." Well, he gets the hint an' buys another box of moth balls. Imagine: Then he gives me the wink an' breezes away.

Well, then Mr. Big Guy Quinley starts up a big blow. I mustn't flirt with the customers—I'm dis-playin' the merchandise all wrong—I didn't dust off the counter. Sayin' everythin' he can to see me squirm.

Certainly I let him have it. While he's foamin' up all over the place, I says, "Wrap it up, boss man, but I ain't buyin'. I've been soaked behind camphor so long I feel like a racoon coat—without a rah rah." Well, that left him limp. An' then I says—

Also By

Clay Franklin

ANYBODY WE KNOW?

I STEP FROM A FAMOUS STORY

IT'S MY TURN

PEPPS AT PEOPLE

BLUE YONDER
Kate Aspengren

Dramatic Comedy / Monolgues and scenes
12f (can be performed with as few as 4 with doubling) / Unit Set

A familiar adage states, "Men may work from sun to sun, but women's work is never done." In Blue Yonder, the audience meets twelve mesmerizing and eccentric women including a flight instructor, a firefighter, a stuntwoman, a woman who donates body parts, an employment counselor, a professional softball player, a surgical nurse professional baseball player, and a daredevil who plays with dynamite among others. Through the monologues, each woman examines her life's work and explores the career that she has found. Or that has found her.

THE OFFICE PLAYS
Two full length plays by Adam Bock

THE RECEPTIONIST
Comedy / 2m, 2f / Interior

At the start of a typical day in the Northeast Office, Beverly deals effortlessly with ringing phones and her colleague's romantic troubles. But the appearance of a charming rep from the Central Office disrupts the friendly routine. And as the true nature of the company's business becomes apparent, The Receptionist raises disquieting, provocative questions about the consequences of complicity with evil.

"...Mr. Bock's poisoned Post-it note of a play."
– *New York Times*

"Bock's intense initial focus on the routine goes to the heart of *The Receptionist's* pointed, painfully timely allegory... elliptical, provocative play..."
– *Time Out New York*

THE THUGS
Comedy / 2m, 6f / Interior

The Obie Award winning dark comedy about work, thunder and the mysterious things that are happening on the 9th floor of a big law firm. When a group of temps try to discover the secrets that lurk in the hidden crevices of their workplace, they realize they would rather believe in gossip and rumors than face dangerous realities.

"Bock starts you off giggling, but leaves you with a chill."
– *Time Out New York*

"... a delightfully paranoid little nightmare that is both more chillingly realistic and pointedly absurd than anything John Grisham ever dreamed up."
– *New York Times*

CPSIA information can be obtained at www.ICGtesting.com
Printed in the USA
LVOW04s2144080215

426215LV00010B/84/P